FILM MAKING ON A BUDGET

By Liane Mahugh

Film Making on A Budget

ISBN: 9798378773602

Imprint: Independently published

Version 2.1
Originally Published: February 2023
Revised: September 2025

Cover created by Canva

DISCLOSURE AND PERMISSIONS

This book is for educational purposes.

No part of this book may be reproduced, or stored in a retrieval system, or transmitted in any form or by any means, electronic, mechanical, photocopying, recording, or otherwise, without express written permission of the author.

This book is licensed for your personal enjoyment only. This book may not be re-sold to other people.

You may not use this book to endorse. or imply endorsement of, products or services not already endorsed within the book. If in doubt, or if you require specific permission not covered by the above, please email the author at: liane.mahugh@gmail.com

Thank you for respecting the hard work of this author.

LEGAL NOTICE

Table of Contents

INTRODUCTION

Lights, Camera, Action: How to Make Your First Film Without Breaking the Bank

Picture this: you've got a dream of making your own movie. The lights, the camera, the thrill of yelling "Action!" It's all bubbling up inside you. Then reality sneaks in, whispering tales of people who've spent their life's savings only to end up with a film that looks like a home video shot on a shaky phone. This doesn't have to be your story. With this guide, you'll discover how to make your big directorial splash for far less cash than you'd expect. Plus, you'll learn how to attract support and funding from real industry insiders. Yes, it's a harsh world to break into, but impossible? Absolutely not!

If you've spent years glued to the screen, analyzing every camera movement and soaking up cinematic magic, you might be itching to call "Cut!" from behind the camera yourself. It's easy to catch the filmmaking bug, but turning that passion into a finished film? That's where the adventure begins.

First things first: directing isn't just about having an eye for visuals or being able to boss people around (though a bit of leadership never hurts!). You'll need to juggle storytelling, people management, and project wrangling—from the first spark of an idea to the final frame of your movie. Yes, it's going to mean hard work, late nights, and maybe more coffee than you thought humanly possible. But if you stick with it, you'll wind up with a finished project you'll be bragging about for years. Maybe it'll even launch an exciting new career. Remember, difficult doesn't mean dull. In fact, the process is likely to be one of the most enjoyable, rewarding, and unforgettable experiences of your life.

This book is your roadmap from wild-eyed dreamer to bona fide filmmaker. We'll walk you step-by-step through how to get your project off the ground and keep it on track. You'll learn how to plan smart, dodge rookie mistakes, and sidestep the classic traps that trip up first-time directors.

Once your plan is set, it's time to roll up your sleeves and dive into production. You'll learn how to keep your crew motivated and productive (hint: happy crew, happy shoot), how to coax unforgettable performances from your actors, and how to shape the atmosphere on set so that everyone's giving their best. When you finally call "That's a wrap!", the next phase begins. Post-production is where all the magic comes together. Here, you'll gain insider tips on editing, making your footage shine, and adding those finishing touches that will captivate audiences and keep them engaged.

So, if you're ready to take your love of movies from the couch to the director's chair, fasten your seatbelt. This book is here to help you chart your course, dodge the potholes, and bring your vision to life, without going broke. Let's get rolling!

PART ONE

PRE-PRODUCTION

CHAPTER 1

Motivation and Goals in Filmmaking

Let's start with a simple truth: the magic of movies doesn't happen by accident. Whether you're shooting a small backyard adventure or embarking on an ambitious festival entry, planning is the backbone of any film project. It might surprise you just how much time, thought, and energy need to be invested long before anyone yells "action!" In fact, the more you plan, the smoother your production will run. It's almost like Murphy's Law was written with filmmakers in mind: anything that can go wrong will go wrong, unless you've planned for it.

Think about it for a moment. If you cut corners during the planning stages, you're almost guaranteed to run into confusion and chaos later. From equipment breakdowns to missed shots, the cost of poor preparation grows exponentially. Rather than hoping for the best, it's far wiser to anticipate problems and have solutions ready. Roll up your sleeves, grab a notebook, and start charting your course. The roadmap you create now will be your lifeline throughout the filming process.

The Investment: Filmmaking Isn't Cheap

Now, let's talk money. There's no way around it: making movies costs cash. Even a so-called low-budget production will chew through resources faster than you'd expect. You'll need to budget for locations, gear, crew, permits, props, costumes, food, and a mountain of other expenses. And here's the kicker. Every minute you spend in production comes with a price tag. It doesn't matter if the camera is rolling or you're waiting for a cloud to pass; the clock is ticking, and your budget is shrinking.

This is where careful planning pays off. For every hour you spend with actors under the lights, you'll likely need to dedicate six to eight hours beforehand for mapping out the details. Pre-production is where your dreams become reality, or at least where you figure out how to make the most of what you have. It's the stage where you lock down your script, scout locations, finalize your shot list, and make tough decisions about what you can afford to do, and just as importantly, what you can't.

Don't let the numbers scare you. Instead, let them motivate you to be resourceful. If you're working with limited funds, every dollar counts. This is the time to get creative, recruit friends, repurpose household items as props, and call in favours. Just remember: the smaller your budget, the more crucial it is to plan wisely, so you don't find yourself stuck halfway through with no money and a half-finished film.

Defining Your Goals

Once you've grasped the financial realities, it's time to get personal. Ask yourself, what's your motivation for making this film in the first place? Are you looking to capture a few fun memories with friends, test your creative limits, or lay the groundwork for a future career in filmmaking?

If your plan involves running around with a camera on the weekend, just letting loose and seeing what you come up with, that's fantastic. There's no pressure to produce a blockbuster, and you're free to experiment as much as you like. Sure, your final product might not look like something from the silver screen, but that's perfectly okay. The most important thing is to enjoy yourself and learn something along the way. Just keep an eye on your spending. If you're not planning to monetize your project, it's wise to track costs and avoid financial regrets.

But let's say your ambitions are bigger. Maybe you want to produce a short film or even dream of tackling a feature-length movie to show at festivals. This is the classic go big or go home approach, but it's not for the faint of heart. Entering the festival circuit presents a significant opportunity to showcase your skills, network with other filmmakers, and potentially catch the attention of investors. Short films, especially those under thirty minutes, are a great starting point. They're more manageable, require fewer resources, and there are plenty of festivals that specialize in showcasing shorts.

If you're considering a feature-length film, here's some advice from industry veterans: think twice before making this your debut. The scale and complexity of a feature can be overwhelming, especially when you're finding your footing as a director. Funding one is often the biggest hurdle. Unless you have deep pockets or a major backer, it's an uphill battle. That's not to say it can't be done; there are inspiring stories of first-time directors defying the odds and making a splash with their debut features. Just know that these are the exception rather than the rule.

Innovative Alternatives: Trailers and Portfolio Pieces

If a full feature feels out of reach, there's a smart middle ground that many aspiring filmmakers use. Create a trailer for your envisioned feature-length movie. Think of this as your calling card. A short, three-to-four-minute showcase that packs all the energy, style, and storytelling chops you'd put into the main project. A well-made trailer effectively demonstrates your vision, showcases your ability to assemble a talented crew, and proves you know how to captivate an audience visually. It's the perfect way to attract investors or collaborators who might help bring your larger project to life.

This approach has several advantages. First, it's far less expensive than shooting the whole movie. Second, it allows you to test out ideas and work with your team before committing to a much bigger undertaking. Third, it provides you with something tangible to showcase when pitching your film at festivals, seeking grants, or meeting with potential backers.

Setting Realistic Expectations: Fun or Fortune?

At the end of the day, it's crucial to be brutally honest with yourself. Are you hoping to make money from your film, or are you treating this as a valuable learning experience? Both paths have their merits. If you're chasing financial success, you'll need to be even more diligent about your planning, budgeting, and marketing efforts. You'll also need to understand the business side of filmmaking: distribution, rights, contracts, and all the nitty-gritty details that turn creative passion into profit.

If, on the other hand, your goal is to gain experience, build your skills, and connect with other creative minds, that's equally valid. Many filmmakers treat their early projects as a form of film school in the real world. And there's nothing wrong with that. You'll learn lessons that can't be found in textbooks, and you'll develop a sense of what works (and what doesn't) through hands-on practice.

Throughout this book, you'll find strategies and advice for both types of filmmakers. While the focus is often on creating movies that have the potential to generate income, the concepts and techniques we discuss apply to anyone who wants to bring their vision to life, regardless of the outcome.

The Road Ahead

If you remember just one thing from this chapter, let it be this: filmmaking is a journey, not a destination. Whether you succeed or stumble, each project brings its own set of challenges and rewards. Planning, budgeting, and clarity of purpose are your best friends. The more time and effort you invest in preparation, the smoother your shoot will go, and the better your chances of bringing your creative dreams to life.

Before you start rolling the camera, take a few days (or weeks) to consider your goals thoroughly. Write down what you want to achieve, how much you're willing to spend, and what measures you'll take to overcome the inevitable obstacles. Discuss it with your team, seek advice from experienced filmmakers, and don't be afraid to adjust your plans as you gain more insight.

Whether you're making a movie for fun, for fame, or for fortune, the habits and skills you develop now will serve you well for years to come. Gather your ideas, set your sights, and get ready to create something unforgettable. Remember, every great film starts with a single spark of motivation, and the courage to follow it all the way to the end credits.

CHAPTER 2

Crafting the Right Script

When it comes to making a film, one of the earliest and most important steps you'll face is getting your hands on a solid script. Whether you're the type who loves to jot down ideas late at night, someone who prefers to delegate writing duties, or you're lucky enough to stumble upon a script that fits your vision perfectly, the journey of turning an idea into a shootable screenplay is a real adventure. It doesn't matter if you're planning a blockbuster or a cozy indie project; having the correct script is what steers your film from concept to completion. While there are whole shelves packed with books that detail every step of script development, there are a handful of fundamental principles that can make your life a lot easier as you figure out how you want to approach this crucial part of filmmaking.

Should You Write the Script Yourself?

Let's start with the biggest question: Should you take on the challenge of writing the script yourself? It might seem tempting—after all, nobody knows your story quite like you do, and you probably have a specific vision in mind for how it should unfold. But there's something to be said for keeping a bit of distance from your project. Getting too close to your own work is a classic pitfall for many first-time filmmakers. When you're both the writer and the director, there's a risk of blurring the lines between the original narrative and your cinematic interpretation. That confusion, where words and images collide, can end up showing on screen in ways you never intended.

Now, don't get me wrong, there are exceptions. Some people can write and direct with seamless clarity, crafting exactly the film they imagine. But it doesn't hurt to be cautious. One common issue is that it's easy to become overly fond of your own writing. When you write for yourself, every line feels precious, every scene feels essential, and you can start to lose sight of what really moves the story forward. The truth is, most screenwriting is about eliminating the fluff and focusing on what matters: advancing your plot, developing your characters, and keeping the audience engaged.

Screenwriting is, in many ways, an exercise in minimalism. You'll probably find yourself having to cut large portions of your original draft, even scenes or bits of dialogue that you personally adore. It's part of the process: whittling your story down to the elements that really sing on screen. If you're able to step back and edit with a critical eye, writing your own script can be a rewarding experience. You have the advantage of tailoring every aspect to your strengths. Say you live near a port or shipyard, for example, you can set your story there, using the unique location to ground your narrative in a way that would be impossible for someone in a landlocked city. When you write your own script, you also have flexibility for plot twists and production tricks that fit your resources, helping you avoid unnecessary expenses.

Practical Tips for Self-Writing

If you decide to dive in and write yourself, here's a practical way to get started: use note cards. Many directors swear by this method. Start by blocking out your scenes and ideas on individual cards. You don't need to write dialogue at this stage, unless you have a killer line you just can't let go of. Instead, think of these cards as a rough roadmap. They help you visualize how your story will unfold, making it easier to spot gaps or pacing issues before you've even begun the screenplay itself. Later, you can transform this outline into a full script or a detailed storyboard, whichever works best for your creative process.

Don't forget that writing is rewriting. Your initial draft is just the beginning, so be prepared to revise, cut, and reshape your work. Ask for feedback if you can and try to approach your own writing with the same objectivity you'd use for someone else's. The goal is always the same: to produce a script that's tight, compelling, and ready to be brought to life on screen.

Bringing in a Professional Writer

Often, especially if you're new to filmmaking, you'll find yourself needing some professional help to turn your ideas into something that resembles a movie script. Even if you've got a rock-solid plot outline, nothing can sink a promising film faster than clunky, unconvincing dialogue. That's where bringing in an experienced writer can make all the difference.

It's not just about technical skill, either. Film is a collaborative art form, and the person you choose to write your script needs to understand and share your vision. Sometimes, you'll find excellent writers who aren't seasoned scriptwriters but can still polish your draft and help you create a finished product that's far more marketable. Their contribution isn't just about putting words on paper; it's about shaping your story in ways you might never have considered.

Finding the Right Fit

When you're searching for a writer, look for someone open to collaboration and flexible enough to adapt to your needs. Have conversations about your concept, your desired tone, and any must-have elements for your film. The right writer will ask questions and suggest improvements, and together you'll develop a script that's stronger than anything you could've done alone.

And while it's not fun to think about, be sure to get everything in writing. A contract that outlines the rights and responsibilities of both parties is essential. This isn't about being distrustful. It's about protecting everyone involved. If things take a turn for the worse—maybe you and your writer can't agree on the direction, or life throws a curveball—it's good to have an explicit agreement so you can part ways amicably. Without a contract, misunderstandings can quickly turn ugly, and you risk losing not just time and money but also a potentially great story.

The Collaborative Process

Working with a professional writer can be a learning experience. You'll see firsthand how someone else interprets your ideas, and you'll probably find yourself inspired by their approach. The process isn't always smooth. There may be debates over character motivations or the best way to resolve a plot point, but that's all part of the creative dance.

Don't be afraid to give feedback, but also be open to suggestions. Sometimes, what feels essential to you might not have the impact you think. A good writer will help you see your project from new angles, ensuring the final script is not only well-written but also primed for production.

Optioning an Existing Script

Another path you might explore is optioning or purchasing a script that's already been written. This approach can be particularly appealing if you're feeling stuck or want to avoid the writing process altogether. But it comes with its own set of challenges, especially for first-time filmmakers.

To begin with, purchasing a script can be costly. Experienced screenwriters spend months, or sometimes years, perfecting their work, often going through multiple rewrites to nail down every detail. It's perfectly reasonable for these writers to expect fair compensation for all that effort, which can make purchasing a script a stretch on a tight budget.

Creative Solutions for New Filmmakers

But don't lose hope! There are creative ways to make this option work, even if you don't have piles of cash to spend. For example, you might offer a writer a share of future profits rather than a large upfront payment. Some newer screenwriters are eager for opportunities to see their work produced; for them, having a film credit or a completed project to showcase is worth more than immediate payment. In these cases, you might be able to get a script for a song, especially if you're willing to work with someone less experienced.

Now, working with inexperienced writers requires care. You'll need to be extra picky about the script you choose. Take the time to review multiple drafts and ensure that the story, dialogue, and pacing meet your standards. If you're willing to put in the effort, you can transform a rough gem into a filmable script with a bit of work.

Your Rights as the Script Owner

One key point to remember: When you buy a script, you own it outright. That means you have the right to change anything you want, without having to consult the original author. If a section doesn't work for your vision, don't let yourself be pressured into keeping it. Sometimes a script contains a brilliant idea that needs a tweak here, a rewrite there, to become truly usable. You can handle this task yourself or bring in another writer to help, giving you maximum control over your project.

Don't be afraid to negotiate. Writers know their scripts are valuable, but they also want to see them brought to life. If you're honest, respectful, and upfront about what you can offer, you might be surprised how flexible people can be, especially in the indie film world.

Making the Final Decision

So, which route should you take? Write the script yourself, hire a writer, or purchase a pre-made script? There's no universal answer, but here are a few things to keep in mind as you decide.

- Know Your Strengths: If you're a natural storyteller with a knack for dialogue, writing might feel right. If you struggle to turn ideas into coherent scenes, consider getting help.

• Think About Time and Budget: Writing (or rewriting) a script takes time—sometimes months. Be realistic about your schedule and resources.

• Consider Collaboration: Film is rarely a solo endeavour. Even if you write your own script, bringing in others for feedback can elevate your work.

• Protect Yourself: Contracts aren't just for big Hollywood productions. They're smart business for anyone who wants to avoid headaches later.

• Be Flexible: The perfect script may need to change to fit your budget, location, or cast. Stay open to new ideas and opportunities.

Turning Words into Film

Getting the correct script is a bit like finding the perfect pair of shoes. It needs to fit not just your creative vision, but also the practical realities of your production. Sometimes, you'll have a clear idea from the start; other times, you'll discover what you want through collaboration, trial and error, or even serendipity.

Whichever route you choose, remember that the script is the backbone of your film. It guides every other decision—from casting to location to editing. Treat it with care, and don't be afraid to put in the work or seek help when you need it. With patience, flexibility, and a willingness to learn, you'll end up with a screenplay that's ready to make the leap from page to screen.

And if nothing else, keep in mind that every great film started as a script—sometimes scribbled in a notebook, sometimes hammered out by a team, and sometimes stumbled upon when least expected. Your journey to the correct script is uniquely yours, and it's a vital part of the filmmaking adventure. Take your time, explore your options, and get ready to bring your vision to life. The words you shape today might be the scenes audiences remember tomorrow.

CHAPTER 3

Storyboards: Bringing Your Vision to Life

Storyboards are one of the filmmaker's most powerful tools.
They're the bridge between your imagination and what ends up on
the screen. If you're looking to share your ideas with collaborators,
producers, or even your cast, sketching out your vision is the most
effective way to do so. Let's be honest: not all of us are gifted
artists, and that's perfectly fine! If you have some drawing skills,
don't hesitate to put pencil to paper and start illustrating your ideas.
On the other hand, if your stick figures leave you feeling a little
self-conscious, there's absolutely no shame in hiring someone to
help you out. Whether you draw them yourself or commission an
artist, remember that storyboards don't have to be masterpieces
worthy of a gallery. Their real job is to convey the mood,
movement, and action you want to capture.

Why Storyboards Matter

Think of storyboards as the blueprint for your film. They serve as
a visual outline, helping everyone involved in the production get
on the same page. With storyboards, you're turning abstract ideas
and written words into something tangible. It's much easier to
pitch your film, discuss ideas, and fine-tune your shooting script
when everyone can see what you're aiming for. Plus, storyboards
help clear up misunderstandings before you're on set and the
cameras are rolling. They're your chance to work out visual
storytelling problems ahead of time so that the production can run
more smoothly.

How Detailed Should Your Storyboards Be?

When you're putting together your storyboards, there's no strict rule dictating how many frames you should create for each scene. The number depends entirely on the complexity of your scenes. Maybe you're dealing with a simple exchange between two characters. One or two frames might be enough to show the main action. But if you have a car chase, a dramatic fight, or a montage, you might end up sketching twenty frames or more to capture each moment and camera angle. Every visually distinct shot should get its own frame. These images will help you plan camera placement, movement, and how each actor fits into the scene.

The goal is to condense the action of an entire shot into a single drawing. Don't worry if your sketches look rough or unfinished. You're not creating a graphic novel. You're making a tool for your film. Each frame should clearly show what's happening, whether it's a wide shot of a landscape, a close-up of a character's reaction, or a dynamic action shot. Try to avoid cluttering your frames with too many details. Instead, focus on what's essential. The characters, their positions, the camera angle, and any movement need to be highlighted. Sometimes, arrows can be used to indicate a pan, tilt, or tracking shot, while other times you might need to show how two scenes connect visually.

No Artistic Skills Required

No one expects your storyboards to be works of fine art. All that matters is that they're easy to understand. If you're working with a team, your storyboards should be clear enough that anyone can look at them and instantly grasp what's happening. You can add simple notes or directions in the margins, like "Camera pans left" or "Character walks toward the door." These little cues help guide your crew and cast, but the images themselves should do most of the talking. The goal is to establish a visual language that everyone can easily understand.

It's also worth noting that storyboards aren't just for directors. Directors of photography, set designers, and even the actors will use them to plan their work. The clearer your storyboards are, the smoother your production will go. The images serve as reference points that everyone can turn to when they have questions about blocking, shot composition, or movement.

Using Storyboards to Plan Your Shoot

One tried-and-true technique is to physically cut out each storyboard frame and arrange them in order. Spread them out on a table or pin them to a board, and you'll have a literal roadmap of your film. This hands-on approach is surprisingly practical for visualizing the flow of your scenes and shots. It helps you identify possible problems with continuity, pacing, or staging before you set foot on location. You can shuffle frames around, insert new ones, or discard unnecessary shots. By seeing the entire sequence laid out, you get a big-picture view of your project that's hard to achieve by just reading your script.

This method not only helps you, but it's a fantastic way to communicate with your cast and crew. When actors can visualize the sequence of events, they're better able to understand how their actions fit into the bigger picture. The crew can use storyboards to plan lighting setups, camera movements, and even stunts or special effects.

Adding Flexibility to Your Plan

Although storyboards are a brilliant planning tool, please don't treat them as set in stone. Film is a collaborative and dynamic process, and things can change quickly on set. Weather, locations, or actor availability might force you to rethink some shots, and that's completely okay. Storyboards are there to guide you, not restrict you. Being willing to adapt your visual plan will help you make the most of your production environment and unexpected opportunities.

Some filmmakers even refine their storyboards during the production process. If a particular shot doesn't work as planned, you can redraw it or adjust on the fly. The key is to maintain a clear visual roadmap for the remainder of your shoot.

Going Digital

While paper and pencil are classic, many filmmakers now use digital tools for storyboarding. Apps and software allow for quick editing, sharing, and rearranging. You can collaborate remotely with artists or teammates, making changes in real-time. Digital storyboards, complete with movement indicators and colour-coding, can make things even clearer. Whether you keep it old-school or embrace new technology, the key is that your storyboards help everyone get on the same page.

Making Your Vision Visible

Ultimately, storyboarding is about transforming your ideas into something that everyone can see and build upon. Whether your sketches are rough doodles or polished illustrations, their purpose is to communicate your story and provide visual direction for your shoot. Don't be afraid to ask for help, experiment with different styles, or adapt your boards as your film evolves. The more precise and informative your storyboards are, the better your film will be. Every great movie starts with a vision, and every vision is easier to realize when it's drawn out for all to see.

CHAPTER 4

Cast, Crew, and Location

If you've ever watched a great movie and marvelled at the way all the pieces come together, you've probably wondered how it happens behind the scenes. The truth is that filmmaking is a massive group effort. It's a blend of vision, talent, sweat, and a bit of luck. For the director, it's like being the captain of a ship: you set the course, but the journey depends just as much on your crew and cast as it does on your own decisions. In this chapter, we'll break down the nitty-gritty of assembling the people who'll bring your movie to life, and how to make the most of the location where the magic will happen.

Film Is a Team Sport

Let's start with the basics: film is anything but a solitary pursuit. Sure, you might have written the script alone, and you might have the clearest vision in the room, but it won't mean much if you can't communicate that vision to your team and collaborate with the people who have the skills to make it real.

Your cast and crew are more than just resources; they're collaborators, creative partners, and, sometimes, the voices of reason when things get tough. Whether you're operating with a big studio budget or shooting guerrilla-style on the weekends, remember this: the people working with you are there to help build something special. They're offering not just their time, but often their labour, expertise, and creative suggestions. And let's not forget, your name isn't the only one that will roll in the credits.

16

Your goal is to produce a film that everyone involved will be proud to show their friends and family, and happy to see their name attached to.

Low-Budget, High Expectations

If you're working on a low-budget project (many first-time filmmakers are), time becomes your most precious commodity. Every extra hour of shooting means more food, more transportation, more patience. If you're lucky enough to have people volunteering their weekends, you need to respect their schedules. A shoot that drags on for months, or even years, is a tough sell. Most people are willing to pitch in for a weekend or two, but asking for months of commitment, especially for little or no pay, is a significant request.

Plan to make your shoot as short and efficient as possible. That doesn't mean you should rush your work or sacrifice quality for speed. It means you need to be organized, know what shots you need, and stay flexible enough to pivot when the unexpected happens. Before you even call your first rehearsal, think carefully about the scale of your project, what you're really asking of your team, and how you'll keep everyone motivated throughout the process.

Finding People Who Know Their Stuff

You might be surprised to discover how many seasoned professionals are willing to lend a hand for the right project. For many people in the business, especially those early in their careers or between bigger gigs, working on an independent film can be a valuable opportunity. It's a way to network, stretch their creative muscles, or lend a hand to something they believe has potential. Sometimes, experienced crew members treat such a project like a working audition, giving you their best so you'll have a stronger pitch for future funding or sponsorship.

When you set out to assemble your crew, aim high for those key positions. A talented Director of Photography (DP) or a skilled sound technician can significantly elevate the quality of your film.

If you manage to recruit these pros, you'll be able to focus more on what matters most to you—telling your story, directing your actors, and keeping your project moving forward.

Professionals are often in high demand, and it's not unusual to lose crew members to better-paying gigs at the last minute. It's not personal, it's just the nature of the business. Be prepared to adapt. Trust your instincts, listen to recommendations from your team, and don't be afraid to promote a hard-working amateur or shuffle roles as needed. The show must go on, and sometimes a shakeup leads to unexpectedly great results.

Ideally, each department (camera, lighting, sound, art, etc.) will have someone experienced at the helm, even if the rest of the team is less seasoned. Sometimes you'll find that a pro DP is happy to work with a semi-pro gaffer and a handful of enthusiastic amateurs, especially if they've collaborated before. The most important thing is to build a team that works well together and is invested in making your film a success.

When Amateurs Get the Job Done

Not every job on set requires years of specialized training. For many roles, all you need is someone reliable who's willing to pitch in. Maybe it's keeping curious bystanders out of the shot, holding up a reflector, or running errands. Don't underestimate the number of small but crucial jobs that need to be done, especially on a busy shoot.

For these positions, enthusiasm and reliability often outweigh experience. If you're clear about what you need and provide a little direction, most people can learn the basics quickly. Friends, family, and eager film buffs can fill non-critical roles. Ensure that someone on your team is present to supervise and answer any questions.

This principle also applies to your actors. Not every part needs a seasoned pro, especially for non-speaking or background roles. Maybe you need a crowd for a street scene or a few extras at a party. Don't be afraid to ask friends and family for help. Just ensure that everyone knows what's expected and keep things light and enjoyable.

Choosing and Casting Your Actors

Casting is a mix of art and practicality. You want actors who not only look right for the part but who also bring your characters to life with authenticity and presence. It's tempting, especially for first-time directors, to step in front of the camera themselves. There's a certain appeal to starring in your own movie, but for most people, it's better to resist. Cameos are one thing. Think Alfred Hitchcock's blink-and-you-miss-it appearances or Stan Lee's beloved Marvel moments. But making yourself the lead is a different story. It's easy to lose perspective, and chances are, your energy will be better spent behind the camera.

When casting, consider what each role requires. Sometimes, the best person for a part isn't the one with the most acting experience, but the one who fits the character. If you're casting a superhero, they need to look the part, regardless of how well you know them. Consider the character's energy, age, and physicality.

That said, acting experience does matter. It doesn't have to be film or TV experience. Stage actors often make excellent film actors, and it's a relief to know your cast won't freeze up the moment you call "action." If they're open to direction, you can guide them toward the performance you envision.

Most cities, even smaller ones, have a surprising number of actors eager to build their resumes, especially for interesting projects. Post a casting call at local theatres, colleges, or online forums. If you have a compelling concept or a unique script, you'll likely have more volunteers than you expected. In fact, it's often easier to find actors willing to volunteer their time than it is to find crew, so use that to your advantage.

Location Scouting – Bringing Your Story to Life

Where's all this going to happen? Even if you're planning to shoot everything against a green screen, your actors and crew need somewhere to work. Selecting the correct location can add production value, alleviate logistical headaches, and ensure your shoot runs smoothly.

There are two main options: building a set or shooting on location. Each has its pros and cons. Sets offer control over lighting, sound, and weather, but can be expensive and time-consuming to build. Real-world locations, by contrast, provide authenticity and atmosphere without the cost of construction, but they come with their own set of challenges.

If you're trying to keep costs down, your best bet is to find a warehouse, vacant building, or other inexpensive space you can temporarily transform. Sometimes, a team member will know someone with access to a cool space, such as a restaurant after hours, a friend's apartment, or even an unused office. Networking pays off here, so don't hesitate to ask around. The more creative you get, the more interesting your film can look without draining your bank account.

Shooting on location, especially outdoors, can be tricky. Weather is always a wildcard, and you may be battling changing light, noise from traffic or passersby, and curious onlookers. Natural light can be beautiful, but it's unpredictable. Have backup plans in place for rain, wind, or other surprises. Consider the practicalities as well: you'll need a place to plug in your gear, areas for your cast to rest, and easy access to restrooms and food.

If you're braving the great outdoors, be mindful of your surroundings. Shooting in rain, snow, or extreme heat adds complexity. Keep your equipment protected, and ensure your team is aware of what they're in for. Sometimes what looks great on screen takes real effort and patience to capture.

Keeping the Project Running Smoothly

Once you've assembled your cast, crew, and found a suitable shooting location, the next challenge is to keep everything running smoothly. Communication is key. Ensure that everyone is aware of what's expected, when to arrive, and how long they'll be needed. Don't take your volunteers' time for granted. Thank people often, ensure they're comfortable, and provide food and regular breaks.

Flexibility is also essential. Things will go wrong. Someone will get sick, a location will fall through, or the weather will refuse to cooperate. Stay calm, keep your sense of humour, and trust your team to help you come up with solutions.

Giving Credit Where It's Due

At the end of the day, your film will reflect everyone who's worked on it, not just you. When the credits roll, you want every person on your team to feel proud of what they've accomplished. If you treat your cast and crew with respect, keep your shoot efficient, and create a positive atmosphere, you'll build relationships that last long after the final scene is shot.

Film is about partnership. Even if you're the driving force, remember that every hand on set contributes to the final product. Approach each project as a collective effort, one where everybody's ideas, energy, and creativity come together to make something greater than any one person could achieve alone.

Assemble your team, find your space, and get ready to create something truly unforgettable. The journey from script to screen is rarely easy, but with the right people by your side and a little bit of luck, you'll get there, and you'll have a blast along the way.

PART 2

WORKING WITH A LIMITED BUDGET

CHAPTER 5

Money Well Spent: Making Every Dollar Count in Your First Film

Making a movie can be more than a little overwhelming. If you're like most first-time filmmakers, your vision is probably epic, but your budget is…not. Don't sweat it. This chapter is here to help you figure out how to spend your money where it really matters, and, just as importantly, how to get what you need for free or cheap by using your smarts, your network, and your creativity.

The True Cost of Filmmaking—and Why It Matters

Let's not sugarcoat things: making a film is expensive. Even the smallest indie projects can rack up costs in ways that surprise you. When you're just starting, it's easy to get lost in dreams of dazzling special effects or that one perfect location, but the reality is that you need to prioritize. Every penny counts, and every spending decision can mean the difference between a polished final product and something that looks (and sounds) painfully amateurish.

The key here is flexibility. You need to be ready to make tough choices about what you spend money on and what you try to obtain by begging, borrowing, or hustling for free. And you really need to understand what each aspect of production is likely to cost before you dive in. With limited funds, you'll often have to let go of specific ideas or get creative with how you execute them. That's not a bad thing; limitations can spark innovation. But it does mean you need to plan carefully.

Camera and Lens Rental

If there's one place where you truly see the value of your investment, it's in your camera and lens package. The camera is, quite literally, your audience's window into your world, and the lenses shape how that world looks. Before splurging on other fancy gear, ensure your camera and lenses are up to the task.

You don't need a trunk full of lenses, just a few excellent ones that suit the style and mood of your film. Many camera rental shops offer packages that include a solid camera body and a couple of quality lenses. Prioritize sharpness and versatility over quantity or novelty. Gimmicky lenses might sound cool, but they rarely deliver what you think they will. Your footage should look clean, professional, and align with the mood you're aiming for. If you want people to take your film seriously, the visuals must look intentional and polished.

When you're shooting on film (yes, some people still do this!), the film stock plays a considerable role in determining the final look. But with digital filmmaking, the camera is just as important as the lens. Older digital video (DV) cameras can undoubtedly get the job done, especially for indoor, controlled shoots, but their technical limitations become apparent in more demanding lighting conditions. For example, they might not be able to handle significant differences between bright outdoor sunlight and darker indoor shadows, and they can struggle to capture the subtle range of colours the human eye sees. If you're planning on shooting outdoors or want a cinematic look, consider renting a high-resolution digital camera, such as the RED or a similar model. It may stretch your budget, but your film will thank you for it.

Getting the Most Bang for Your Buck

Instead of buying, consider renting whenever possible. This gives you access to top-notch gear for a fraction of the price, and you won't have to worry about the hassle of maintenance or storage after the shoot. And here's a pro tip: network with other filmmakers, crew members, or local film schools. Sometimes, people are willing to lend out cameras and lenses, or at least offer a steep discount, if they're excited about your project or want to help you get started.

Sound Capture

If there's one thing that will instantly mark your film as amateurish, it's bad sound. Viewers can forgive a grainy shot or a less-than-perfect lighting setup, but scratchy, echo-filled, or muffled audio will pull them right out of your story. Ironically, we often don't notice good sound. It just feels natural and keeps us immersed in the world you've created. But when it's bad, it's all anyone can talk about.

Capturing clear, crisp sound on set should be just as high a priority as getting beautiful visuals. Yes, you can do a lot to clean up and enhance audio in post-production, but you can't perform miracles. Background noise, echoes, and muffled dialogue are persistent issues that even the best software can't always resolve. It's much better to get it right on the day.

How to Get Clean Audio

Start with the right microphone. A solid, directional microphone (like a shotgun mic) is excellent for isolating voices and cutting out unwanted sounds from the environment. If you're on a tight budget, you can sometimes borrow microphones from your crew, local schools, or even churches with sound systems. Community radio stations might also be a resource.

Sometimes, you can get away with using less expensive omnidirectional mics, especially if you 'treat' your set to dampen sound. Hang heavy blankets or curtains to reduce echoes, or position microphones as close as possible to your actors. Get creative. Don't let a bare, echo-y space ruin your dialogue.

Often, you'll want to use a mixer to combine sound from multiple microphones, one for each main actor in a scene. A basic four-channel mixer is usually sufficient for a small shoot, allowing you to keep your audio tracks organized for later editing. And don't forget the humble slate (digital or otherwise). It helps you keep track of what you're recording (scene, take, reel number, and so forth) and syncs your audio with your video files later.

Makeup: More Than Just a Pretty Face

You might not think makeup is a big deal, but the difference between no makeup and a professional makeup artist can be the difference between a film that looks homegrown and one that feels cinematic and real. Film makeup is a unique art form. It's not just about making people look good; it's about making them look consistent from shot to shot, and realistic in whatever world you're creating.

Ideally, you want to work with someone who has experience in film or theatre makeup. They'll know how to handle everything from subtle touch-ups to wild creature effects, and they'll understand how lighting and camera angles can change the way makeup appears on screen. If you're lucky, you'll find someone willing to work for the cost of materials, maybe to build their portfolio.

A good makeup artist will take reference photos so they can recreate the look exactly for each day of shooting. This is crucial, even for achieving a natural look. Continuity errors are one of the most obvious signs of amateur filmmaking.

If your story requires more advanced makeup, such as for monsters, zombies, or wounds, consider finding someone with specific experience in these techniques. Theatre professionals are often a fantastic resource. Many will have portfolios or demo reels that you can review before making a commitment.

Making Your Film Attractive to Professionals

What can you do to entice a skilled makeup artist to join your project? Offer reasonable shooting hours, a short schedule, and good food (see the next section). Don't forget to highlight the creative challenge and the chance to be part of something fun and unique.

Catering and Craft Services: Feed Your Team, Feed Your Film

One of the best ways to keep your cast and crew happy, focused, and productive is to provide them with good food. Hungry and tired people don't do their best work, and if you want to build goodwill and get the most out of your volunteers, good food is essential.

Catering costs can add up quickly, but this is not the place to cut corners. Good meals, plenty of snacks, and lots (and lots) of coffee go a long way toward making the experience enjoyable rather than gruelling. If you're asking people to volunteer their time and talent, feeding them well is a sign of respect.

How to Save Without Sacrificing Quality

You don't need to provide a fancy dinner every night. Try to schedule your shoot so that you wrap up before dinner time. That way, you only need to provide breakfast, lunch, and snacks. Not only will this save you money, but it also makes it easier to get people to commit to weekend shoots (they'll still have their evenings free).

Never underestimate the power of a hot cup of coffee on set. A medium-sized cast and crew can burn through two pounds of coffee a day, so make sure you're ready for the demand. Have everything people need, from cups to sugar to non-dairy creamers.

Be sure to provide for dietary restrictions. Vegetarian, vegan, kosher, gluten-free, sugar-free. Most people appreciate options, and a little planning goes a long way in keeping everyone feeling included and cared for. Good catering companies can handle this if you ask, but it's always best to double-check and communicate clearly.

Lighting: Setting the Scene (and the Mood)

Lighting might not seem like a glamorous part of filmmaking, but it's essential. The right lights can make a set look like a million bucks—even if it was built for a hundred. Conversely, poor lighting can make even the best sets, and the most beautiful actors look flat, harsh, or unflattering.

Ideally, you'll work with a director of photography (DP) who knows their stuff and has connections to a reliable lighting crew. They may be able to bring some lights with them, or you can tap into your local network to borrow or rent what you need. Film school students are often eager (and affordable) helpers, and they might have access to school equipment you can use at a discount or even for free.

Light, Colour, and Texture

Gels are inexpensive but critical. These are coloured sheets you place in front of lights. They let you change the colour and mood of a scene without renting extra lights, and you can mix and match to create just about any effect you want. Simple, flexible lighting setups will save you time and money, while also giving you maximum creative control.

Building Believable Sets Without Breaking the Bank

You've picked a script with simple sets, but you'll still need to create or manage your filming locations. Whether you're constructing something from scratch or dressing up a real-world location, you've got to think about cost, creativity, and practicality.

The Magic of DIY Set Design

Surprisingly, you can accomplish a lot with basic materials, including plywood, spray paint, paper, glue, and a bit of imagination. "Flats", portable, reusable walls made from plywood, are a staple of set construction, and you can often rent them from theatrical supply companies for way less than buying your own. These typically come with stands and can be repurposed for different scenes or locations. To create different looks, you can cover flats with thin sheets of paper or other materials without damaging the flats themselves.

Remember, a real set doesn't need four walls. Most sets use just two or three, letting you move your camera and lights around easily. Keep it simple. Your focus should be on giving your actors enough space and your crew enough flexibility to work their magic.

If you know a professional set designer who's willing to pitch in, fantastic! Otherwise, enlist friends or local theatre folks, or get creative with what you have. Plan to spend at least one night before the shoot assembling and dressing your set so everything is ready to go.

Pro Tips for Realism

A slick trick is to keep your actors a few feet away from the set walls. This allows you to use the camera's depth of field to keep your actors in sharp focus while the background remains slightly out of focus, creating a professional, cinematic look. Use soft lighting or light from the side to keep harsh shadows from falling on your set walls.

Networking and Pitching

Earlier, we mentioned that you can gain a lot for free simply by pitching your project and networking with people who already work in film, theatre, or related fields. Never underestimate the power of enthusiasm and a good story! People love being part of something creative, and if your project excites them, you might find folks willing to lend you equipment, work for credit, or connect you with other resources.

Reach out to local schools, community theatres, and radio stations. Ask friends and family if they know anyone who might be interested in helping out. Tap into online groups for indie filmmakers. You might be surprised by how generous and supportive the filmmaking community can be when you approach them with respect and passion.

Making Tough Choices: Real-World Advice

So, how do you decide what to spend money on and where to cut corners? Here's a quick checklist:

- Prioritize production value: Spend your money on things the audience will notice—cameras, sound, lighting, and food for your team.

- Don't waste money on gimmicks: Fancy props, wild costumes, and endless special effects can eat up your budget fast. Save your resources for what counts.

- Get creative with what you have: Think outside the box and use what you already have access to—locations, props, costumes, and even people. Creativity often trumps cash.

- Respect your collaborators: Feed them well, treat them professionally, and make the experience fun. Happy people bring their best to the project.

- Plan, plan, plan: The more you prepare in pre-production, the smoother—and cheaper—your shoot will go.

Make Your Money Work for You

Filmmaking on a budget isn't about being cheap; it's about being smart. Invest in what matters, hustle for what you can, and let your creativity fill in the gaps. Every decision is a chance to shape your film and your filmmaking experience. When you spend wisely, build your network, and keep your team inspired and well-fed, you'll find that your money goes a long way further than you ever imagined.

CHAPTER 6

Navigating Production Hurdles

Filmmaking is often romanticized as a world of glitz, glamour, and unlimited budgets. But for most independent creators, the reality is a little less Hollywood and a lot more resourceful. Whether it's your first short film or you're wrangling together another feature with a shoestring budget, being savvy about what to avoid and what to embrace can make all the difference. This chapter serves as your guide to navigating common production hurdles, from wardrobe woes to tracking shots and the intricacies of obtaining

Costume Conundrums

Let's start with something you, your cast, and your budget will thank you for: straightforward costumes. Elaborate costumes can look stunning on screen, but for most indie filmmakers, they come with a host of complications. Unique outfits tend to be expensive to purchase or manufacture, unless you're lucky enough to have access to a local theatre company's wardrobe archive, but they bring additional headaches. You'll need to maintain them, ensuring consistency between takes and scenes. You must also clean them, sometimes repeatedly, especially if there's any physical action involved.

Think about continuity. Imagine an actor stains their costume during a shoot. If you don't have a backup, reshoots can be impossible. Or consider how an elaborate outfit might look after a few days of filming in the sun, rain, or on a dusty set. Suddenly, that dramatic cape or intricate armour isn't just a visual asset; it's a logistical nightmare.

Write or choose scripts that require as little special clothing as possible. Focus on stories where characters can dress in ordinary, easily replaceable outfits. Jeans and t-shirts, business casual attire, or generic uniforms are not only easier to maintain, but if something happens, you can quickly source replacements without blowing your budget or losing time. If your story absolutely needs a splash of costume flair, get creative. Thrift stores, simple DIY modifications, or borrowing from friends can go a long way. And remember, consistency is key. Take plenty of reference photos and keep a log of costume changes for each character.

Tracking Shots on a Budget

Professional productions often utilize dollies, specialized carts that move cameras smoothly along tracks, to create those sweeping, cinematic shots that give a film a high-end look. Dollies add a sense of movement and production value that static shots can't match. Renting a dolly, especially one that can support a heavy camera, can quickly eat up your budget.

However, don't despair if your bank account isn't ready for a complete setup with a dolly. Enter the humble skateboard. With a bit of ingenuity, you can use a sturdy skateboard as a makeshift dolly. Assign a dedicated operator, practice the moves, and you might be surprised by how smooth your shots can turn out. It's not a plug-and-play solution. Achieving steady, professional results usually takes extra practice and twice as many takes as you'd expect. If you're shooting on actual film, which costs money for every foot you run through the camera, this could add up. Rehearse those moves with a dummy camera or smartphone before you roll film.

Surface quality matters. Any bump, crack, or uneven flooring will show up on camera. Even a sheet of plywood might seem flat to the eye, but it can amplify vibrations that make your shot shaky. When possible, scout locations with naturally smooth surfaces, such as polished concrete, tiled hallways, or hardwood floors. Test everything in advance. If you must lay down your own track, secure it firmly and check for stability before each shot. Sometimes, simple rubber mats can help dampen small shakes.

Don't forget there's an art to handheld shots, too. While dollies are great, sometimes a steady hand and a bit of creative blocking can substitute for gear you don't have. Experiment. You may discover a personal style that's more memorable than any tracking rig.

Jib Arms

If dollies are the workhorses of moving shots, jib arms are the show ponies. These are long mechanical arms that lift and swing the camera for dramatic overhead or sweeping movements. High-budget films often utilize jibs (also known as cranes) to add visual flair and heighten drama. Even a relatively short jib, say eight feet, brings a lot of flexibility.

But with great technology comes great responsibility, and often, great expense. If you decide to rent a jib arm, consider the learning curve. Unless someone on your crew is already familiar, you'll need to dedicate time to master its operation. Practice is essential. Awkward movements or fumbled controls are distracting on film, and safety is paramount. Jibs also take up real estate. They need space to maneuver, both vertically and horizontally, which isn't always feasible in cramped apartments or small sets.

For most small productions, jibs fall into the "nice to have, not need to have" category. It's a much greater testament to your skill as a filmmaker to impress your audience with clever framing, camera placement, and movement rather than relying on expensive gear. If you do feel your story would benefit from a jib shot, see if you can accomplish the effect another way. Sometimes, a ladder, a monopod, or a handheld rig with a stabilizer can get you 80% of the way there. Creativity often trumps equipment.

Location Permits

Let's discuss locations and the associated paperwork. Filming in public spaces (streets, parks, government buildings) usually requires permits from the city or county, and those permits can get expensive fast. Depending on your location, you may need several permits for parking, road closures, crowd control, drone shots, and other purposes. Each piece of paper is another line item in your budget, another potential delay, and another phone call or meeting with local officials.

Anything you can do to minimize the number of permits required is a win. Think strategically about your locations. Can you move a scene from a busy street to a private driveway? Can you set up your crucial dialogue in a backyard instead of a public park? The fewer permits, the less you'll spend, and the easier your shoot will be to manage.

Sometimes, you can bypass the official bureaucracy entirely by finding private sites. Private locations offer more flexibility, fewer restrictions, and often a friendlier process, especially if you have a personal connection to the owner. Semi-private locations are a goldmine for indie projects. Consider college campuses during spring break. These are wide-open spaces, with minimal security, and a lot of architectural variety. Loading docks, trucking company yards, and industrial parks can serve as substitutes for urban settings, highways, or back alleys.

However, tread carefully with corporate campuses. These locations may appear perfect on camera, but big companies often have lengthy, complex approval processes and stringent liability requirements. You may be asked to provide insurance, sign waivers, or even hire security, all of which can balloon your costs and slow you down. Always check the policies before scouting or shooting.

Resourcefulness Over Resources

Making a movie is a balancing act between artistic vision and real-world constraints. It's tempting to chase after eye-catching costumes, Hollywood-grade equipment, and dramatic locations, but the most innovative filmmakers know how to work around limitations without sacrificing story or quality. Keep your costumes simple for the sake of continuity and cost. Get creative with camera movement, whether through skateboards, clever blocking, or handheld rigs. Evaluate whether flashy gear, such as jibs, truly serves your film, or if your storytelling can impress without it. Always be strategic about your locations and permit needs. Private and semi-private sites often offer the freedom you need at a price your budget can afford.

Above all, let your resourcefulness shine. Some of the most memorable and effective films have emerged not from unlimited budgets, but from clever solutions to everyday production problems. Embrace the challenge, seek out practical workarounds, and focus on what makes your story compelling. The less you worry about the things you can't afford, the more energy you'll have to pour into the things that matter: your characters, your vision, and your voice as a filmmaker.

CHAPTER 7

Sponsorship Deals in Independent Film Production

When you're putting together an independent film, whether it's your first short or a micro-budget feature, it's easy to think only the big studios land sponsorship deals or meaningful product placements. However, here's a secret not everyone realizes: even small-scale productions can significantly benefit from the generosity and enthusiasm of local businesses. In fact, you may be surprised just how many of your neighbourhood companies are eager to contribute to the creative process, often in exchange for some good old-fashioned publicity.

The Untapped Potential of Local Sponsorship

Let's start with a simple truth: most small businesses are always looking for fresh ways to get their names out there, and what better way than through film? Even a modest production can offer a unique platform for these companies to reach new customers. Your project doesn't need a six-figure marketing budget or Hollywood connections to attract sponsors. What you need is the willingness to engage with your local community and a little bit of creative thinking.

Say you're filming in a town where there's a popular coffee shop, an up-and-coming brewery, or a beloved bakery. These businesses routinely support local events, donate to schools, and sponsor sports teams. Imagine what happens when you show up at their door and explain your vision and how their brand could be featured in a movie, and their support could help bring your story to life.

Food and Drink: The Secret Sauce of Indie Film Sponsorships

Among all the potential partners, food and beverage companies are often the most open to collaboration. Why? Well, for starters, everyone loves food, and seeing their products on screen creates an instant connection. More importantly, these businesses know that feeding a hungry cast and crew is no small task. They recognize how having their logo in a film can be a win-win.

Here's where things get interesting. Instead of spending precious budget dollars on catering, takeout coffee, or snacks for your team, you can approach a local restaurant, bakery, or even a food truck. Offer them the chance to have their products featured in your film. In return, you get meals or drinks for your set, and they get valuable exposure. It's a simple arrangement, but one that can make a big difference, especially when every dollar counts.

Let's make this practical. Imagine your script has a scene set in a bustling diner. Instead of creating a generic restaurant with no personality, why not collaborate with a real local spot? You could shoot on location, feature their logo on menus, or have your characters order signature dishes. Not only does this add authenticity to your film, but it also establishes a direct connection between the restaurant and your audience.

Even if your story doesn't call for a whole restaurant scene, there are plenty of subtle ways to include local products. Have your characters drinking coffee from branded mugs, snacking on pastries from a local bakery, or enjoying craft sodas with a recognizable label. Product placement isn't just for blockbuster movies. It's a clever way for indie filmmakers to offset costs and build lasting relationships.

Other Creative Sponsorship Opportunities

While food and drink are often the easiest entry points, don't overlook other local businesses. Think about costume shops, florists, hardware stores, gyms, or even car dealerships. If your story features a special prop, wardrobe item, or distinctive location, consider how a partnership might benefit both sides.

Let's say your film needs a classic car for a memorable scene. You could reach out to a local dealership or vintage car club. Offer them a mention in your credits or a cameo of their vehicle, and you might find yourself with the perfect ride, at no cost.

The same logic applies to filming locations. Small businesses with visually interesting spaces, such as art galleries, bookstores, or quirky retail shops, might be thrilled to have their interiors featured. In exchange for letting you shoot there, they get a shout-out in your credits, a logo in the background, or even a nod in the dialogue. Sometimes, they'll even contribute with props, decorations, or assistance with set design.

How to Approach Businesses

If you're new to sponsorship deals, the idea of cold-calling business owners might feel intimidating. But here's the good news: most love working with creative people and are open to hearing your pitch. Here are some practical tips to get started:

- Do Your Homework: Know which businesses in your area have the kind of products or services your production could use.
- Make It Personal: Visit in person, explain your project, and share your passion. A genuine conversation goes much further than a mass email.
- Show the Value: Let them know how their involvement will benefit them. Whether it's on-screen exposure, social media shout-outs, or tickets to a premiere, make it clear you're offering something in return.
- Be Flexible: Some businesses may be able to provide free or discounted products, while others might prefer a small sponsorship fee in exchange for advertising. Negotiate in good faith and find the arrangement that works for both sides.

- Follow Through: Once you've made a deal, honour your commitments. If you promised credit or exposure, ensure it is delivered. Building trust is the foundation for future collaborations.

Product Placement

Don't be fooled into thinking product placement is only for blockbuster hits. For independent filmmakers, it's a valuable tool that can help stretch a tight budget. By working sponsorship deals into your script, you not only save money but also inject real-world authenticity into your film.

Think about your favourite scenes from movies and TV shows. How often do you see characters sipping coffee with a recognizable logo, or eating at a familiar chain restaurant? Those moments feel genuine because they reflect the real world. The same can be true for your project, whether you're filming a quirky romantic comedy, a tense drama, or a coming-of-age story.

Building Relationships for the Long Term

One of the best aspects of seeking local sponsorships is the opportunity to form lasting relationships within your community. Businesses that support your film become invested in your success. They're likely to promote your finished project on their own social media channels, display posters in their shops, or host screening events. Over time, these partnerships can grow, making future productions easier and more rewarding.

Be Creative, Be Bold

Getting local sponsorships isn't about selling out; it's about collaboration. It's about recognizing that great art often needs a helping hand, and that your neighbours might be more supportive than you expect. Whether you're seeking sandwiches for your crew, costumes for your actors, or a memorable location for that pivotal scene, reach out to the businesses around you. You might find that a bit of creativity and a willingness to ask can make all the difference in bringing your vision to life.

Next time you're working on a script, keep an eye out for scenes where you can naturally incorporate products or services from local sponsors. With a thoughtful approach and a spirit of partnership, you'll not only save money, but you'll build a network of support that lasts far beyond your final shot.

CHAPTER 8

Legal and Labour Pitfalls in Filmmaking

Making a film, whether it's a modest indie project or a larger production, is a thrilling journey that blends creativity, determination, and teamwork. But along this path, many less glamorous, yet crucial, details can make or break your film's future. One of the most critical areas that often trips up new filmmakers is navigating the legal and labour landscape. It might not be as exciting as selecting camera lenses or building sets, but overlooking these aspects can spell disaster for your project, regardless of how visionary your storytelling may be.

Let's break down some of the key steps you ought to take if you want to dodge legal landmines and labour troubles that could halt your film in its tracks.

Why Release Forms Matter

Imagine spending months, maybe even years, working on your film, pouring your heart and soul into every frame, only to discover you can't legally show it to anyone. This nightmare scenario can happen, and often does, simply because you didn't get the proper release forms signed.

A release form is essentially a contract where the person being filmed permits you to use their image, voice, or other identifying characteristics in your film. This applies to everyone who appears in your movie, no matter how briefly. Even someone who wanders through the background for a split second could come back later and object to being included if you don't have their written consent. That's all it takes to get your film tied up in legal knots, possibly preventing you from ever finishing or releasing it.

So, what's the solution? Make it your policy to have every single person who will appear on camera sign a release form before you start shooting. Have extra copies on set, keep them as organized as you would your shot list, and get signatures before the cameras roll. It might seem tedious, but it saves you from headaches, legal bills, and disappointment down the line.

The Case for Incorporation and LLCs

Let's say your film is shaping up to be something special. Maybe it's headed for festivals or even a commercial release. Or, on a more sobering note, maybe there's an action scene or a tricky stunt that carries some risk. In these cases, simply working as an individual, or even as an informal group, isn't enough to protect you.

That's where forming a company comes in. You have several options, but two of the most popular are incorporating (creating a corporation) and forming a Limited Liability Company (LLC). These structures serve as a legal shield between you as an individual and your film project. If something goes wrong, if someone gets hurt on set, or if there's a dispute about payment or ownership, having a corporation or an LLC means your personal assets (like your car, house, or savings) are generally protected from lawsuits or debt collection related to the film.

Incorporating your film is straightforward, but the specifics depend on your state. Most states require at least two or three people to sign on as founders, and a modest fee is usually involved. You'll fill out some simple paperwork, often called articles of incorporation, and file them with the appropriate state office. Once that's done, your film project exists as its own legal entity.

LLCs are often the default choice for filmmakers, as they offer liability protection with less paperwork and more flexible management structures than traditional corporations. You'll want to check the specific rules in your state, as details can vary, but in many cases, you can even form an LLC in a different state if one of your principal team members lives there or if it offers more favourable terms.

The bottom line: If your film is anything more ambitious than a home movie, you should at least consider forming an LLC or corporation. It's one of those grown-up steps that can save you a world of trouble later.

To Insure, or Not to Insure?

Insurance may not be the most thrilling topic, but it's an essential consideration for anyone making a film. At its core, insurance is about managing risk. It helps cover costs in the event of unexpected events, such as property damage, accidents, or injuries on set. If you have insurance, you're not only protecting yourself, but you're also more likely to be allowed to film at a wider variety of locations, since many property owners or municipal offices require proof of coverage before they'll let you in.

Let's get real, though: insurance isn't cheap. If you're working with a tight budget, especially if you're financing the whole project yourself, it can feel like an expense you can't afford. This is where the legendary "guerrilla filmmaking" approach comes into play: shooting quickly, loosely, and under the radar, often without permits or insurance. Plenty of classic indie films have been made this way, but it's essential to realize what you're risking. If someone is injured, or if there's property damage, you can be held personally responsible. That's not just a slap on the wrist, but possibly a lawsuit that could put your financial future in jeopardy.

If you have external funding, maybe from investors, grants, or a production company, insurance is non-negotiable. It'll be baked into the budget from the start, and you'll likely have no say in the matter. Even if you're on your own, though, it's worth considering at least minimal coverage, such as general liability insurance, to give yourself a safety net.

Protecting Your Film and Yourself

There is a reason legal and labour issues are such a big deal in filmmaking: a single misstep can spell disaster, no matter how brilliant your script or how talented your cast and crew. The best advice is to be proactive. Get that release form signed, investigate setting up an LLC or corporation, and seriously think about insurance. These steps might not feel like part of the creative process, but they're what make the creative process possible.

By covering your legal bases and protecting your team, you not only safeguard your project but also demonstrate professionalism and respect for everyone involved. While it might be tempting to focus only on the artistic side, don't neglect these crucial details. Your future self and your film will thank you.

CHAPTER 9

Making Challenging Scripts Work Through Tone

There's a golden rule that floats around the hallways of film schools and among fresh-faced directors stepping onto their first set: when you're just starting, steer clear of complicated scripts. This isn't about being afraid of a challenge, but rather about being strategic. Stories that venture into the realms of science fiction, fantasy, or historical drama often come accompanied by significant demands. Think elaborate set designs, period-specific costumes, and the relentless need for meticulous script supervision. For many, the advice is to leave these ambitious projects for a time when you've gained a bit more experience (and perhaps a larger budget). But here's the twist: you can sometimes make these complex scripts not only doable, but enjoyable if you're smart about setting the tone of your film.

Tone, in film, isn't just about mood. It's the underlying flavour, attitude, or emotional hue that colours every scene, line, and character. It's what makes a gritty crime drama feel tense and dangerous, or a quirky comedy feel light and spontaneous. Tone is the director's secret weapon, and if you know how to wield it, you can take a story that seems logistically overwhelming and turn it into something manageable, relatable, and, most importantly, watchable.

Let's break this down with some examples. Say you're obsessed with science fiction. You've read all the classics, you've dreamed up entire worlds, and you've got a script burning a hole in your drawer. The reality, though, is that sci-fi can be a bear for a novice filmmaker. It typically requires special effects, futuristic sets, and technology that appears convincing. If you go for a straight-up sci-fi epic as your first film, you might find yourself drowning in challenges. But what if you flipped the genre on its head?

Imagine making your sci-fi debut as an existential comedy. Suddenly, the pressure to create a photorealistic alien planet or seamless spaceship interiors falls away. You can shift the focus onto clever dialogue, absurd situations, and the humour found in the characters' reactions to otherworldly events. The audience becomes more invested in the laughs and the philosophical undertones than in whether your space station looks like it cost a million bucks. By choosing a comedic or satirical tone, you're not just side-stepping expensive and time-consuming production hurdles; you're giving your film a unique flavour that sets it apart from the crowd.

But the magic of tone isn't only for sci-fi. Crime dramas, for example, are notorious for requiring gritty urban landscapes, shadowy back alleys, and believable criminal activity. If you don't have the budget or resources to recreate the mean streets of New York or a smoky jazz club from the 1940s, you can use tone to your advantage by embracing noir aesthetics. Noir, as a genre, is defined by its use of darkness, both literal and metaphorical. You can use black as your primary colour, bathing your sets in shadows and using minimal lighting to evoke danger and intrigue. This isn't just a stylistic choice; it's a practical one. Suddenly, you don't need expensive sets or locations. A simple room with the proper lighting setup can become a menacing interrogation chamber, a clandestine meeting spot, or a place where secrets unravel. By leaning into the noir tone, you transform your limitations into strengths.

Of course, setting the tone isn't just a magic wand you wave over your script. It requires thought, intention, and a clear idea of what you want your audience to feel. When you begin production, the tone you choose will guide countless decisions, from costume design to camera angles to the way your actors deliver their lines. It's about creating a cohesive atmosphere that supports your story and makes the challenges of your script seem less daunting.

Let's say you're working on a period piece. Typically, this would mean tracking down authentic costumes, building sets that resemble those of another century, and ensuring every detail is accurate to the time. But what if you decided to set your story in a stylized version of history? Perhaps you use exaggerated costumes and props, or you shoot in black and white, lending the film a dreamy, timeless quality. You can incorporate elements of magical realism, letting the audience know upfront that this isn't a strict historical recreation, but rather a fable or an allegory. This approach not only saves you money and effort, but it also allows you to play with creative visual language that highlights your story's themes.

The best part about using tone to tackle difficult scripts is that it puts the power back in your hands. Instead of feeling boxed in by what you can't do, you start focusing on what you can do. You find ways to make your limitations work for you, enhancing the story instead of detracting from it. Audiences are surprisingly forgiving when a film is confident in its tone; they're willing to accept a cardboard spaceship or an obviously fake mustache if the story has heart, humour, or emotional resonance.

In practical terms, this means that as you head into production, you should be thinking about tone at every stage. When scouting locations, ask yourself if the space supports the mood you want to create. When designing costumes, consider whether bold colours or subdued palettes will help set the atmosphere. When working with actors, discuss the underlying tone of each scene so their performances reinforce the feeling you're aiming for. Every choice should be filtered through the lens of tone.

Directors who understand the power of tone often find that they can make even the most ambitious scripts work. They're not afraid to take risks—to turn a potential weakness into an opportunity. They see the big picture, knowing that audiences connect with story and character before they notice the specifics of set design or special effects.

If you're a first-time director dreaming of tackling a script that seems too big, too strange, or too complicated, don't let logistics kill your ambition. Instead, spend some time thinking about which tone would best serve your story, your resources, and your audience. Maybe you turn your fantasy epic into a whimsical comedy, or your gritty drama into a minimalist, dialogue-driven piece. By making tone your ally, you'll find ways to bring even the wildest scripts to life—no matter what your budget or experience level.

When you're staring down a script that scares you, remember tone isn't just an artistic flourish. It's your tool for transformation, your ticket to creative freedom, and your secret to making the impossible possible. Set the right tone, and watch your film become everything you imagined, and more.

PART 3
PRODUCTION

CHAPTER 10

Film or Digital?

Collecting Your Raw Footage: The Essential First Step

Let's talk about the very foundation of making your film, whether you're a budding director, a resourceful indie filmmaker, or someone with a phone and a dream. Before the magic of editing, before you can wow your audience with seamless storytelling, you need raw footage, and plenty of it. This is your lifeblood, the raw clay you will shape and sculpt. If you miss capturing those crucial moments now, especially if you're working on a shoestring budget (and let's be real, most of us are), that's it. You can't go back and fetch what you never shot. Treat every filming opportunity as your golden hour. Be prepared to grab just one more take, even if everyone looks tired and the sun's about to set. Sometimes, that last shot turns out to be the magic ingredient you didn't realize you needed.

Pay Attention to Both Detail and the Big Picture

While you're out in the field gathering footage, it's easy to get swept up in the technical aspects of framing, focusing, and hitting record. But don't forget to step back and consider what your audience will experience when they watch your film. Think about the story you're telling, not just in terms of individual shots, but as a complete, immersive experience. Are you capturing the right mood and energy? Are you zeroing in on the details that will make your story stand out, while also ensuring the overall vision is coming together? Sometimes, it's the tiny choices that matter. The glint of sunlight on a character's face, the way the wind moves through the trees. These can stick with viewers long after the credits roll.

People Management

Here's something that might surprise you. You can spend months learning how to frame the perfect shot, how to light a scene, how to use the latest camera gear. However, when production begins, technical skills often take a back seat to people skills. Managing your cast, crew, and even the random passersby who wander into your shooting location is an art. Can you keep everyone motivated, organized, and happy? Can you give direction while listening to feedback and managing stress? Your ability to handle people, to encourage, to smooth over conflicts, to keep spirits up. can make or break your shoot. While you're practicing camera moves, don't forget to build those leadership muscles too.

Film Versus Digital: The Modern Dilemma

Let's move on to the big question: Should you shoot with film or digital? This debate has been raging for years, but it's gotten especially interesting lately. Once upon a time, film was the undisputed king of moviemaking, prized for its dreamy colours, deep shadows, and organic warmth. But digital technology has come a long way. Today, the latest digital cameras boast resolutions and dynamic ranges that can rival, and sometimes even surpass, what film can deliver. That means the choice isn't as clear-cut as it once was.

For many filmmakers, the decision comes down to a matter of personal taste. Some swear by the classic look of film, while others prefer the convenience, flexibility, and cost-savings of digital. But before you make your call, there are some tried-and-true observations to keep in mind.

The Unique Appeal of Film

Film has a reputation for producing stunning results, especially in high-motion outdoor scenes. There's something almost magical about the way film captures sunlight, movement, and natural colours. The warmth and texture of film are tricky to replicate digitally. If you're shooting action sequences outside, whether it's a chase through city streets or a dance in a sun-dappled meadow, film can give you an edge.

However, film comes with a hefty price tag. Not only do you have to buy fresh film stock (and yes, freshness matters. Old film can lose its vibrancy and reliability), but you also must pay for development, processing. Sometimes, extra takes are needed if things don't go perfectly. This can quickly eat up your budget, especially for indie projects and student films. Plus, there's always a risk: sometimes the film doesn't develop quite the way you hoped, and the colours or clarity aren't what you envisioned. Unlike digital, you have less control over tweaking the footage after the fact.

The Advantages of Digital

On the flip side, digital cameras offer a level of flexibility and practicality that's hard to beat. With digital, you aren't limited by the length of your film rolls or the looming cost of each new take. If you miss a shot, you can instantly review it and try again. The quality of digital footage today is truly impressive, with some cameras capable of shooting in 4K or even higher resolutions. You can capture crisp, vibrant images in almost any lighting condition, and post-production editing is far simpler. Want to tweak the colour, brighten up a shadow, or cut together a rapid-fire montage? Digital makes all this possible with just a few clicks.

Digital gear is also generally lighter and easier to handle, which is a relief if you're working with a small crew or shooting guerrilla-style. The instant feedback you get from digital monitors lets you adjust your setup on the fly, and you don't have to worry about the logistics of shipping film to a lab for development. For anyone working on a budget, the cost savings are substantial.

Weighing the Pros and Cons

So, how do you decide which route to take? Begin by considering the look and feel you're aiming for. If your project is all about nostalgia, atmosphere, or capturing the timeless beauty of a landscape, film might be the best approach, provided you can afford it. If speed, efficiency, and creative flexibility are your top priorities, digital is likely the smarter choice.

Both formats have their strengths and quirks. Film offers a classic, cinematic aesthetic that's hard to duplicate, but it's expensive and unpredictable. Digital is reliable, fast, and budget-friendly, with plenty of room for experimentation and correction. Some filmmakers even mix the two, using film for key moments and digital for the rest, to get the best of both worlds.

Making the Most of Your Resources

Whether you're working with film or digital, the key is to stay resourceful and open-minded. Always be prepared to capture extra shots, especially when inspiration strikes or when your actors deliver a perfect performance. Don't be afraid to experiment. Sometimes a quick, unscripted moment ends up becoming the highlight of your project.

Pay close attention to your team and make sure everyone is on the same page. The energy and cooperation of your cast and crew are just as vital as your technical setup. Remember, filmmaking is a collaborative adventure, and the best results come from striking a balance between artistic vision and practical know-how.

Crafting Your Vision

At the end of the day, there's no one-size-fits-all answer to the film-versus-digital debate. It's all about your goals, your resources, and the story you want to tell. Gather as much raw footage as possible, keep your creativity sharp, and remember to manage your team with patience and care. Whether you're chasing the golden glow of film or the high-definition power of digital, what matters most is the passion and commitment you bring to the process.

So, grab your camera, whatever type it may be, and get shooting. Your story is waiting to be told, and every frame you capture brings you one step closer to making it unforgettable.

CHAPTER 11

Essential Sound Equipment

If you've ever sat through a movie and found yourself distracted by fuzzy voices, background hums, or dialogue that feels miles away, you know just how important sound is to film. In fact, the quality of your audio can make or break your entire feature. Whether you're a first-time filmmaker or a seasoned pro gearing up for another shoot, nailing your sound setup is an art and a science that deserves just as much attention as your camera work and lighting. So, let's dive into the world of essential sound equipment, breaking down what you need, why you need it, and how to make sure it all works together to support the story you're trying to tell.

Why Sound Matters

You've probably heard that people will forgive poor visuals before they'll forgive bad audio. There's a reason for that: sound is your invisible storyteller. It sets the mood, conveys emotion, and brings your characters to life. If your audience struggles to hear what's happening or must endure distracting background noise, you'll quickly lose their engagement, no matter how stunning your visuals are. The last thing you want is for your hard work to go unnoticed simply because your sound didn't measure up. Before you even pick up a camera, it's worth taking a step back and planning your audio setup with the same care you give to every other part of your production.

Microphones

Let's start with the most obvious piece of gear: the microphone. There's a whole world of microphones out there, and picking the right one isn't just about grabbing the first model you see at the store. Each microphone has its own strengths, weaknesses, and ideal applications. If you want crisp, clear dialogue and immersive ambient sound, you'll need to understand the types of microphones available and how to utilize them effectively.

Lavalier Microphones (Lav Mics)

For scenes where your actors are mostly stationary or the action is minimal, a lavalier microphone is a top choice. These tiny microphones can be discreetly clipped onto clothing, hiding in plain sight while capturing every word spoken. Most lavaliers today are wireless, meaning they connect via a transmitter, often tucked away under clothing or behind the back, so they don't show up on camera. However, wireless transmitters can be a bit bulky. If you plan to shoot wide, full-body scenes, it's worth thinking about how and where to conceal the transmitter.

Wired lavaliers also exist, and they're often less susceptible to interference and noise. They tend to be more affordable as well. If your scene doesn't require a lot of movement (or you can hide the cable effectively), a wired lavalier might be the better option. The key is knowing your scene and selecting the mic that best suits it.

Directional Microphones and Boom Poles

Not every scene can use a lavalier, especially when the action gets physical. Action sequences, dances, or even more intimate moments where clothing might not be an option for hiding a mic. This is where the boom microphone comes in. A boom setup involves a directional microphone mounted at the end of a long pole (the boom), allowing you to capture audio from above, below, or beside your actors without getting in the way of the frame.

Operating a boom isn't as easy as it looks! The pole can stretch up to 14 feet and get heavy fast. Your boom operator needs strength and stamina, not to mention an eagle eye for staying out of the shot.

If you notice the boom dipping into your footage, it might be time to find a more experienced operator or make your frame lines more straightforward. Communication between the director, camera crew, and boom operator is essential to ensure everything runs smoothly.

Choosing the Right Mic for the Scene

Every microphone has an ideal range and placement. Understanding the sweet spot where your mic sounds best is essential. Too far away, and you'll pick up only echoes and background noise. Too close, and you risk making your actors sound unnatural or even picking up unwanted sounds, such as breathing or clothing rustling. Before filming any scene, test your microphones, check their ranges, and experiment with placement. Don't wait until the day of the shoot; get familiar with your gear ahead of time so you're ready for anything.

Microphone Cables

While microphones get all the glory, cables are just as necessary. After all, if your cables aren't properly installed or maintained, you could spend an entire day shooting only to discover the audio is unusable. That's a heartbreaker for any filmmaker, and a mistake you definitely want to avoid.

Quality Matters

Not all cables are created equal. Low-quality cables can introduce hiss, static, and other forms of interference into your recordings. Investing in sturdy, shielded cables can save you a lot of headaches in the long run. Ensure the connectors are solid and fit tightly into your equipment; loose connections are a common cause of lost audio.

Routine Checks and Maintenance

Even the best cables can fail if neglected. Develop the habit of regularly checking your cables, especially before and during shoots. Look for fraying, kinks, or worn insulation, and listen for any signs of interference or dropouts. Periodic checks during filming are a smart move. A glance at your connections between takes can catch problems before they ruin your footage.

Setup Tips for Success

When laying out cables, keep them organized and out of the way. Use cable ties or gaffer tape to secure them, especially in high-traffic areas. Avoid running cables parallel to power lines, which can introduce noise. And whenever possible, keep spares on hand. Having an extra cable or two can be a lifesaver if something goes wrong during a shoot.

Sound Software

Capturing great audio is half the battle; the other half is making it shine in post-production. This is where sound editing software comes into play. Good software empowers you to tweak, rearrange, and refine your recordings, transforming raw audio into polished and professional results.

Editing Basics

With sound editing software, you can adjust the order of dialogue, layer in sound effects, and balance audio levels for maximum clarity. For example, if a noisy siren interrupts your perfect take, editing software lets you swap out that unwanted sound for clean ambient audio. This flexibility can mean the difference between salvaging a scene and having to reshoot it from scratch.

Noise Reduction and Ambient Sound

No matter how careful you are, unwanted sounds will sneak into your recordings. Maybe it's a car horn, a barking dog, or just the hum of the air conditioner. Modern software includes powerful noise reduction tools that can help minimize these distractions, preserving the integrity of your scene. If you've taken the time to record ambient sound separately, you can use it to mask or replace intrusive noises, creating a seamless audio experience for your viewers.

Advanced Features

Don't be afraid to explore the advanced features of your sound software. From equalization and compression to reverb and spatial effects, today's programs offer a whole toolbox for refining your soundtrack. Experiment with different settings, mix levels, and add subtle effects to enhance mood and atmosphere. The more you learn about your software, the more control you'll have over your final product.

Bringing It All Together

Each element—microphones, cables, and software—plays a critical role in crafting your film's soundtrack. Skimping on any one part can lead to disappointing results. Imagine watching a beautifully shot movie where the dialogue is muffled or out of sync, or where background noise overpowers the story. Chances are, you'll tune out quickly.

That's why it's worth taking the time to assemble a solid sound kit, testing everything in advance, and staying vigilant during your shoot. Your audience may not notice when your audio is perfect, but they'll certainly notice when it isn't.

Pride in Your Sound

Great sound doesn't happen by accident; it's the result of thoughtful planning, careful execution, and creativity in both recording and editing. When you take pride in your audio, it shows in the final product. Viewers are more likely to engage with your film, appreciate its subtleties, and remember it long after the credits roll.

But beyond technical excellence, sound offers a unique opportunity for artistic expression. Don't be afraid to experiment with different microphones, cable setups, or editing techniques. Try layering in ambient sounds to heighten tension or create atmosphere. Play with volume and effects to evoke emotion or underscore key moments. The possibilities are endless—and each choice you make brings your vision to life in a new way.

Tips and Tricks for Filmmakers

- Plan Ahead: Scout your locations for potential sound issues, like street noise or echoing rooms. Bring extra gear to address unexpected challenges.

- Test Everything: Set up your microphones and cables before the shoot. Perform a few test recordings and listen back with headphones to catch any issues early.

- Communicate Clearly: Make sure your crew knows the frame lines and understands how to avoid sound equipment making an accidental cameo in your shots.

- Stay Flexible: Not every scene will go as planned. Be prepared to adjust your equipment and techniques to achieve the best sound possible, regardless of the situation.

- Keep Learning: Technology evolves quickly. Stay updated on the latest gear and software, and don't be afraid to ask for advice from fellow filmmakers.

The Soundtrack of Your Success

Sound is much more than a technical necessity—it's a storytelling tool, an emotional driver, and a way to set your film apart. By investing in the right equipment, taking care with your setup, and mastering your editing software, you'll give your audience the immersive experience they crave. Whether you're shooting your first indie project or your latest blockbuster, a focus on sound will pay off in every frame.

The Soundtrack of Your Success

Sound is much more than a technical necessity—it's a storytelling tool, an emotional driver, and a way to set your film apart. By investing in the right equipment, taking care with your setup, and mastering your editing software, you'll give your audience the immersive experience they crave. Whether you're shooting your first indie project or your latest blockbuster, a focus on sound will pay off in every frame.

So, as you gather your gear and prepare for your next shoot, remember sound deserves respect. Take pride in your audio work, keep experimenting, and your films will resonate with viewers in ways you might never expect. After all, a movie isn't just seen, it's heard. Make sure what your audience hears is every bit as powerful as what they see.

CHAPTER 12

Practical Lighting Tips for Filmmakers on a Budget

Rethinking Lighting: Creativity Over Cash

Most aspiring filmmakers don't have the bottomless budgets of Hollywood directors. You might dream of working with the latest professional lighting rigs, but when your wallet says otherwise, it's time to get resourceful. The good news? You can achieve impressively professional results with a bit of ingenuity and a keen eye for alternatives. Among all the production expenses, lighting is one of the best places to get creative and save big.

The Price of Professional Lights—and the Alternatives

One of the first things you'll notice when researching equipment is just how expensive lighting can be. Professional-grade lights run anywhere from $200 to $1,000 apiece, and that's not including stands, modifiers, and accessories. For many indie filmmakers, students, or creators just getting started, those numbers are simply out of reach.

There's a world of affordable lighting solutions waiting to be discovered. In fact, many filmmakers have found ways to mimic the results of high-end gear using budget-friendly tools. For example, halogen work lights are a fantastic alternative. You can often pick them up at your local hardware store for under $40 each, and when paired with a basic $20 light stand or "light tree," you're well on your way to building a setup that'll impress.

Bright Ideas: Halogen Lights and Light Trees

What's the deal with halogen lights? These workhorse fixtures, designed for construction sites and garages, offer a high wattage output, typically around 500 watts per bulb. For context, many professional "key lights" in film production are rated at 1,000 watts, so using two halogen lights together can give you roughly the same power as a single pro model.

The real trick is combining these affordable lights with a simple light tree or stand. You don't need anything fancy; even a sturdy tripod from a hardware store will do. Mount your halogen units, plug them in, and voilà: you have a versatile, budget-friendly light source that can be moved around and positioned as needed.

This approach frees up your budget for other essentials, such as camera gear, sound, props, and more. It's a great example of how thinking outside the box can help you stretch every dollar and still deliver impressive, cinematic results.

Lighting for Different Situations

Let's talk about what you need to light. Not every scene demands the same approach. If you're shooting your actors outside on a sunny day, natural daylight will do most of the heavy lifting for you. In this case, you may only need a little fill light to soften shadows or add a touch of drama.

On the other hand, shooting interiors or nighttime scenes is a different story. In a pitch-black room, you'll need to provide all the illumination yourself, which is where your halogen setup really shines. The beauty of a portable lighting kit is its flexibility. You can adjust, move, and modify your lights to fit the mood and requirements of each scene.

Don't forget that lighting isn't just about making things visible; it's about shaping the look and feel of your film. Soft, diffused light can create a warm and inviting atmosphere, while harsh, directional light adds tension and mystery. By studying lighting both in front of and behind the camera, you'll develop an understanding of how to sculpt your scenes and tell your story visually.

Dialling Down the Intensity

One common issue with budget halogen lights is that they can be a little too powerful. If your scene looks blown out or overly harsh, it's easy to tweak the setup. You have a couple of options:

- Angle the lights: Point them slightly away from your subject to reduce direct intensity. This can also help control shadows and give a softer look.
- Swap the bulbs: Many halogen fixtures allow you to change to lower-wattage bulbs. Try experimenting with 250-watt or even 100-watt bulbs for a subtler lighting effect.

Whichever method you choose, always keep an eye on shadows. Poorly aimed lights can cast distracting or unwanted shadows, which can ruin the continuity and polish of your footage. One helpful tip is to review your shots periodically during filming. Pause, check the monitor, and adjust your lights as needed. This extra attention ensures your scenes look their best.

Bounce Cards

Lighting isn't only about the fixtures themselves. Modifiers play a significant role in creating a professional look. Bounce cards are a classic trick used by filmmakers and photographers to soften and redirect light. They're essentially large, white surfaces that reflect light onto your subject, reducing harsh shadows and creating beautiful, even illumination.

While you can buy professional bounce cards, you don't have to. A simple piece of white styrofoam from your local craft store works wonders and costs just a few dollars. Cut it to size, mount it on a stand, or have an assistant hold it. Instant improvement, minimal expense.

Bounce cards are especially useful for close-ups and interviews, where you want your subject to look their best. They add a touch of polish and can help create that "filmy" look even if you're working with basic gear.

Other DIY Lighting Hacks

Let's explore a few more budget-friendly lighting techniques:

- Household lamps: Floor and desk lamps, especially those with adjustable necks, can be repositioned to provide fill or accent lighting. Experiment with lampshades or fabric to diffuse the light.
- LED strips: Affordable and versatile, LED strips can create interesting background effects or subtle highlights. Many come with dimmers and colour controls for extra flexibility.
- Clip-on shop lights: These hardware store staples are easy to mount and can be fitted with bulbs of different strengths and colours. Attach them to stands, shelves, or even furniture.
- Colored gels: Want to add mood or match a particular colour scheme? Make your own gels by taping colored cellophane or craft paper over your lights. Just be sure your materials are heat-safe!
- DIY diffusers: Soften harsh light by stretching a white sheet, shower curtain, or translucent plastic in front of your bulbs. This scatters the light, giving a natural, cinematic quality.

With a bit of experimentation and creativity, you can achieve almost any look you're after. Don't be afraid to try new things and see what works for you.

Quality vs. Affordability

It's tempting to splurge on professional gear, but remember—great lighting is more about technique than price. Many iconic films have used unconventional or inexpensive lighting setups to stunning effect. Take the time to learn the basics: how to position your lights, how to diffuse and bounce, and how to work with the environment.

As you build your kit, consider slowly investing in higher-end pieces. Perhaps you begin with halogen and bounce cards, then add a softbox or a dedicated video light as your budget expands. The goal is to find equipment that works for you, not just what's trendy or expensive.

Above all, don't compromise on your vision just because you're working with affordable materials. With patience, attention to detail, and a little "DIY" spirit, you can achieve results that rival those shot on big-budget productions.

Lighting on a Shoestring

Filmmaking is all about solving problems and making the most of what you have. When it comes to lighting, a limited budget can push you to be more creative and resourceful. By exploring alternatives such as halogen work lights, bounce cards, and DIY modifiers, you can create beautiful, professional-looking scenes without breaking the bank.

Remember, every filmmaker faces limitations. What sets great creators apart is their ability to adapt and innovate. Experiment, learn, and trust your eye. With these lighting tips, your film will look polished, your actors will shine, and your audience will never guess you pulled it off for a fraction of the cost.

CHAPTER 13

Making the Most of Production Time

Time and money are two sides of the same coin, especially when you're making your first film. While that old saying "time is money" might sound like a cliché, you'll find it's never truer than when you step onto a set, surrounded by lights, actors, crew, and the ticking clock. Whether you're filming a short indie or wrangling a feature-length script on a shoestring budget, managing production time is an art form all its own. How do you ensure that every precious minute and every dollar go as far as possible? The answer lies in thoughtful planning, adaptability, and a healthy dose of leadership.

Why Planning Each Day Counts

Let's face it, most first-time filmmakers don't have the luxury of unlimited funds. You're probably working with a lean budget, and every decision you make has ripple effects across the day. This means you need to sweat the details from sunrise to sunset. Your day starts with something as simple as a casting call and ends with the final "wrap" of the day. In between, every moment counts.

If you've put in serious effort during pre-production, such as scouting locations, locking down your cast, storyboarding your shots, and organizing the logistics, then your day-to-day worries on set will shrink. But even with rock-solid pre-production, curveballs can, and will, happen. Perhaps an actor falls ill, the weather changes, or a vital prop goes missing. These are the moments where your skills as a leader and your ability to make quick, tough decisions really shine. You may need to cut scenes, rework your script, or adjust the shooting order. Being prepared for the unexpected is essential, and your team will look to you for guidance.

Building and Sticking to Your Production Schedule

Before the cameras roll, you'll have sat through countless production meetings with your core crew: your cinematographer, assistant director, production designer, and maybe a patient friend or two who's handling snacks and morale. Out of these meetings comes one of your most essential tools—a daily production schedule.

This schedule isn't just a vague checklist; it's a detailed map of which shots you need each day, who needs to be on set, and what resources you'll need at each moment. The tighter you stick to this plan, the smoother things will go. Consistency here isn't just about discipline. It's about making sure you have time left in your day for those flashes of inspiration that hit when the light is perfect, or the actors improvise something magical.

That said, don't let your schedule squash your creativity. The magic of filmmaking often happens in unexpected moments. A spontaneous idea, an unplanned shot, or a change in weather that transforms the mood. If you're disciplined about capturing the essential footage first, you'll often find you have a little breathing room at the end of the day. That's when you can experiment, try out new angles, and capture the "wow" shots that give your film its signature style. But remember, that breathing room only appears if you've stuck to your plan earlier in the day.

Why Structure Is Your Friend

Some filmmakers worry that following a schedule will stifle their creative flow but consider the alternative: trying to wrangle a cast and crew without any sense of timing or order. Imagine calling your actors the morning of a shoot and hoping they'll all be available at the exact moment you need them. Chances are, you'll end up with a lot of space, wasted hours, and maybe your main character stuck in traffic or missing entirely.

This chaos is compounded the larger your cast and crew become. The more people involved, the more challenging it becomes to coordinate everyone's needs and availability. With a clear schedule in hand, you can give everyone advance notice of when they're needed. That not only helps your team plan their own lives but also builds trust. People appreciate having the information they need to show up and give their best.

Arriving on set with a whole crew, only to find that your lead actor is nowhere to be seen because you forgot to send the schedule. Suddenly, you're burning through daylight and your budget, wishing you'd just made that extra phone call or sent an email the night before. It's a lesson you only need to learn once.

Punctuality Sets the Tone

Being the director means leading by example. If you expect everyone else to be on time, you need to be the first one in, ready to go (and preferably with coffee in hand). Showing up before your team isn't just about logistics—it's about respect. When the crew sees you arriving early, sweating the details, and suffering those early mornings right alongside them, it builds a sense of camaraderie.

Coffee is key. Trust me, it's a universal language on set. If people must be up at dawn, ensure the caffeine is flowing and the breakfast snacks are easily accessible. And don't forget about the makeup and costume department—they need to be set up and ready before any actors arrive. If they're still laying out brushes and costumes when the talent walks in, you'll start your day behind schedule.

A film set runs on a schedule tighter than most people experience in their everyday lives. If one crew member is late or missing, the entire operation can grind to a halt. People end up standing around, waiting for something to happen. That's not just frustrating; it's expensive. Your goal should be to build in enough time at the start of the day for everyone to get settled before you dive into shooting. The earlier your call time, the better your chance of staying ahead.

Leaving on time matters just as much as starting on time. While you can keep shooting until you get the perfect take, respecting people's time is critical. If your cast and crew know you're serious about getting them out at a reasonable hour, especially if they need to be back early the next day, they'll be more focused and energetic throughout the shoot.

Handling the Unexpected

Even with the best-laid plans, things can go wrong. Perhaps a location falls through at the last minute, a camera breaks, or an actor gets stuck in traffic. Your job is to remain calm and roll with the punches. Sometimes, you'll have to make tough calls: dropping a scene, rewriting dialogue, or reordering your shot list. These moments are stressful, and they're also the times when your leadership really matters.

One way to minimize chaos is to build some flexibility into your schedule. Allow a little extra time for unexpected events. If you finish a scene early, use that extra time to experiment or get ahead on the next setup. If something takes longer than expected, don't panic. Focus on what's most important for the day and adjust as needed. Communicate clearly with your team about any changes so no one feels blindsided.

Communication Is King

Smooth productions hinge on clear communication. Make sure everyone knows where they need to be, what's happening next, and what to expect throughout the day. Use call sheets, group texts, or walkie-talkies, whatever works best for your team. The goal is to keep everyone informed and engaged, allowing you to move efficiently from shot to shot.

If you're running behind, don't be afraid to update the schedule. Let your cast and crew know if lunch will be later or if you'll need to adjust your plans. People are far more understanding when they see what's going on. Surprises are inevitable, but confusion can be avoided with a few quick updates.

Respecting Everyone's Time

Time management isn't just about keeping your film on track, it's about respecting the people who make it happen. Every cast member, crew member, and volunteer is giving you their time and energy, often for little or no pay. Showing that you value their contribution by running an efficient set, starting and ending on time, and keeping people informed goes a long way toward building a positive atmosphere.

If you're running late, communicate the reason and provide a realistic estimate of when you expect to be finished. Thank them for their patience and do your best to make the wait as comfortable as possible (again, coffee and snacks can be helpful). If you consistently respect their time, you'll build a reputation as someone people want to work with again.

Finding Balance: Structure vs. Spontaneity

The best filmmakers know how to strike a balance between discipline and creative freedom. Stick to your schedule for the shots you absolutely need but be ready to break out and experiment once those essentials are covered. That's where you'll often find the magic—those moments you couldn't have planned that bring your film to life.

It's also worth remembering that sometimes, less is more. If a scene isn't working or you're falling behind, don't be afraid to cut it. Maybe you don't need every shot you planned, and perhaps the story will be stronger for it. Trust your instincts and be willing to adapt.

Wrapping Up the Day

As the end of the day approaches, focus on getting the last shots done and preparing your team to leave. A smooth wrap means everyone knows when they can start packing up, what needs to be cleaned, and who's responsible for what. Provide clear instructions and extend thanks to everyone for their hard work.

If something didn't get shot, don't beat yourself up. Make notes about what needs to happen the next day and communicate that to your team. The most important thing is to maintain high morale and ensure everyone returns home safely.

Managing production time wisely isn't about sacrificing creativity for the sake of the clock. It's about creating a structure that allows your vision to flourish, your team to work efficiently, and your film to come together without unnecessary stress. With careful planning, respect for everyone's time, and a willingness to adapt, you can turn even the tightest schedule into an opportunity for creative success. And remember—coffee is your friend, communication is your superpower, and every minute saved is a chance to make your film just a little bit better.

CHAPTER 14

Keeping Your Crew Happy and Busy

Managing a film crew is a unique challenge, but in many ways, it shares common ground with other forms of team management you may have experienced in the past. The core goal is straightforward: get the very best out of your people while they're with you, so your production runs efficiently, stays creative, and maintains high morale. Of course, production sets have their own quirks, and one of the most familiar sights is a cluster of actors or crew members standing around waiting for the next shot to be ready. While a bit of downtime is inevitable, you can do a lot to keep things humming along with thoughtful planning and solid leadership.

Let's discuss how to keep your crew not only busy but also happy and motivated throughout the shoot, while ensuring your set is a place where creativity flourishes and everyone's efforts are valued.

Minimizing Idle Time

No matter how well you plan, there will always be moments of downtime, especially for actors who often find themselves waiting as technical teams adjust lights, cameras, and sound. It's almost a rite of passage in filmmaking. Standing around in costume, sipping lukewarm coffee, and waiting for the all-clear. But while you can't eliminate all idle time, you can minimize it with a bit of strategy.

Start with a clear shooting schedule. Make sure each department—camera, lighting, sound, art, and so on—knows what's expected of them and when. The more information you share ahead of time, the fewer surprises on the day. Allow your department heads, such as your director of photography and production designer, the autonomy to manage their own teams. They know their jobs, so trust them to get the job done.

Meanwhile, use the natural ebb and flow of the shoot to keep your actors engaged. While the crew is setting up for the next shot, take the opportunity to rehearse upcoming scenes with your cast. This serves a couple of purposes: it keeps your actors in the zone, and it means you can iron out any last-minute problems in the script or blocking before the camera rolls. It's a win-win.

The Importance of Rehearsals

One of the best ways to keep everyone on track is to hold rehearsals with your actors a few days before shooting begins. These sessions are invaluable for working out not just lines, but also movements, character relationships, and emotional beats. You won't be shooting your script in the order it appears on the page; film production almost always works out of sequence, usually starting with wide shots and gradually moving into close-ups and more emotional moments. This can be unclear even for seasoned actors, so rehearsing in advance helps them adjust to this rhythm.

Use these rehearsals to clarify expectations. Walk your actors through the schedule, explain the logic behind the shooting order, and let them ask questions. The more comfortable and prepared they are, the smoother things will go when the pressure is on. And don't forget to include some time for your actors and crew to get to know each other. It helps foster a sense of camaraderie that will pay off when things get stressful.

On-Set Engagement

When shooting days run long (and they almost always do), it's easy for energy to flag. Your role as director or team leader is to keep spirits high. Small gestures go a long way: a word of encouragement, a genuine thank you, or even just a box of donuts during a late-night shoot can make all the difference. If you see someone struggling or getting frustrated, check in with them. Let them know you appreciate their effort and contribution.

It's also essential to keep people informed. There's nothing more demoralizing than standing around with no idea how long the wait will be. If there's a delay, let your cast and crew know what's happening and how long you expect the hold-up to last. Transparency builds trust and keeps everyone feeling like part of the team, rather than just cogs in a machine.

Delegating and Trusting Your Team

One of the biggest challenges, especially for new directors or managers, is learning to relinquish control a bit. You hired your crew for their expertise, so let them use it. Whether you're working with seasoned professionals or enthusiastic newcomers, trust is key.

Micromanaging every little detail will only slow you down and sap your energy. Instead, focus on the big picture and let your department heads handle the specifics. This doesn't mean you're hands-off or oblivious to what's going on; it means you're allowing your team to shine in their areas of strength. Keep an eye out for potential problems and be available to answer questions, but resist the urge to meddle in every decision.

Film is a fundamentally collaborative art form. The best productions are those where each person—whether setting up lights, dressing the set, or wrangling extras—feels a sense of ownership and pride in the final product. Make it clear that you value input from all corners. Invite suggestions, listen actively, and consider new ideas, even if you don't end up using them. Sometimes the best solutions come from unexpected places.

Communication: The Secret Ingredient

Open communication isn't just about logistics; it's also about fostering a positive, creative environment. Make it known from day one that everyone's voice matters, from the grips and gaffers to the makeup artists and production assistants. If someone shares an idea, listen to them. You're not obligated to explain every decision or adopt every suggestion, but making your crew feel heard will earn their respect and loyalty.

As a first-time director, you might feel pressure to have all the answers, but remember that your crew can be an invaluable resource. They bring their own experiences, technical know-how, and creative insight to the table. When making a decision, be confident, but remain open to feedback. If you decide against a suggestion, you don't have to justify your reasoning to everyone. Acknowledge the input, thank them, and move forward.

Leading with Respect and Confidence

Ultimately, managing a crew is about balance: balancing preparation with flexibility, authority with openness, and vision with practicality. Be clear about your goals and expectations but leave room for spontaneity and adaptation. The unpredictable nature of film production means things will go wrong. Equip yourself with patience and a willingness to adjust on the fly.

A good leader sets the tone for the whole set. If you're calm and organized, your crew will follow suit. If you panic or become impatient, negativity can ripple through the team. Model the attitude you want to see. Be approachable, decisive, and respectful. Acknowledge mistakes, celebrate successes, and maintain a light mood whenever possible.

Happy Crew, Better Film

When all is said and done, a happy and busy crew is the backbone of any successful film project. By minimizing unnecessary downtime, practicing deliberate rehearsing, delegating tasks effectively, fostering open communication, and leading with respect, you can create an environment where everyone feels engaged and invested. This isn't just good for morale. It leads to better work and, ultimately, a better film.

Keep these basics in mind as you move forward with your production. Trust your people, plan ahead, keep everyone informed and involved, and don't forget to have a little fun along the way. After all, making movies is challenging, but it should also be a rewarding, creative adventure for everyone involved.

CHAPTER 15

Understanding the Role of the Director of Photography

When it comes to making a film, it's easy to imagine the director as the person who's constantly calling the shots, shaping every detail, and overseeing every single aspect of production. But film directing is much more about collaboration and trusting your crew, especially when it comes to the visual look of your movie. That's where your Director of Photography, often referred to as the DP or cinematographer, steps in as a crucial player.

Let's break down why the DP is so important, how their role fits into different types of productions, and what that means for you as a director, whether you're just starting or you've got a few projects under your belt.

What Does the Director of Photography Actually Do?

In simplest terms, the Director of Photography is the person who manages all the visual elements of your film. They're the ones responsible for deciding how each shot is lit, composed, and captured on camera. That might sound straightforward, but it's a massive responsibility that combines technical know-how with a deep sense of artistry.

Your DP is the bridge between your creative vision and the practicalities of capturing it on film (or digital, as is often the case nowadays). They work closely with the director to discuss the look and feel of the story, exploring aspects such as mood lighting, camera angles, lens choices, and the visual flow of scenes. They take your ideas and help make them a reality, using their skills to set up each shot so it looks exactly (or sometimes even better than) what you imagined.

This doesn't mean the director has to be hands-on with every single technical detail. A big part of successful directing is knowing when to step back and let the experts do their thing. The DP is your go-to person for anything related to the camera, lighting, and visual storytelling.

Letting Go and Trusting Your Team

One of the most critical lessons in filmmaking, particularly for new directors, is learning how to delegate. While it can be tempting to micromanage, after all, your movie is your baby, it's almost always better to rely on your team's strengths. The DP is an invaluable resource when it comes to visuals, which frees you up to focus on other aspects of directing, like working with actors, pacing the story, or making creative decisions about set design, costuming, or editing.

On smaller productions, things can get a little more hands-on. Sometimes, due to budget constraints or limited crew, a director might also take on the responsibilities of the DP. This can work, especially for short films or passion projects, but it does add a significant amount to your workload. If you're breaking into filmmaking, juggling these roles might seem feasible at first. However, you'll quickly find that things run much smoothly when you have someone dedicated to managing the camera and lighting setups.

That's why, even in the leanest indie projects, it's worth seeking out an experienced DP if you can. Their expertise can elevate your film in ways you might not expect, and a strong working relationship with your DP can make the entire production process more enjoyable and effective.

Finding the Right DP

If you're new to directing, one of your top priorities should be finding a DP with a solid track record. Think of this role as the artistic engine behind your project, the person who translates your script into images. An experienced cinematographer can offer invaluable advice, pointing out potential challenges, suggesting creative solutions, and helping you avoid common pitfalls.

The best DPs aren't just technically skilled. They're great communicators and collaborators. They know how to interpret your ideas while still bringing their own expertise and vision to the table. They're also able to adapt quickly if things change on set, which, let's face it, happens often in filmmaking.

When you're hiring for this role, don't just look at someone's resume or reel. Have honest conversations about your vision, ask questions, and see how they respond to feedback. The DP-director relationship is a partnership, and you want someone passionate about helping you tell your story in the best way possible.

The DP's Artistic Influence on Your Film

From an artistic standpoint, the DP is one of the most crucial members of your crew. They're not just technicians; they're visual storytellers. Their choices about light, shadow, movement, and colour can dramatically influence the tone and emotion of your film. Sometimes, a DP's creative insights will push your project to places you hadn't considered, making the final product richer and more nuanced.

Consider iconic movies like "Blade Runner" or "The Revenant". The look and atmosphere of those films owes a considerable debt to the cinematographers who helped shape their worlds. Even in a simple character drama or a quirky comedy, a talented DP can use visual language to support the emotional beats and narrative structure, guiding the audience's attention and shaping the overall experience.

The Role of Producers and Assistants

It's easy to get caught up in the artistry of filmmaking, but remember that movies are also logistical projects. While your DP handles the creative side of visual storytelling, your producers, production managers, and assistants help keep things running smoothly from a practical standpoint. They coordinate schedules, manage budgets, secure locations, and handle all the small details that keep the whole operation running smoothly.

A film set is a busy, sometimes chaotic place, and nobody can do it all alone. Lean on your team when you need to. That's what they're there for. Producers are experts at solving problems and keeping everything on track, so you can devote more of your attention to making creative decisions and working with your cast and crew.

Why the DP Is an Essential Collaborator

To sum it all up: as a director, you're the guiding force behind a film, but you don't have to be the expert on everything. Handing over the reins to a skilled DP for tasks like cinematography allows you to focus on what really matters—telling your story, guiding your cast, and shaping the overall vision for your film.

Whether you're stepping onto set for the first time or you've directed a few projects already, understanding and respecting the role of the DP will make your job easier and your film better. Invest time in finding the right person, communicate openly, and trust their expertise. And remember, filmmaking is teamwork at its core. A collaborative art where every crew member brings something essential to the table. With the right DP by your side, you're well on your way to creating something truly memorable.

CHAPTER 16

The First Assistant Director

When you step onto a film set for the first time, it can feel a bit like entering a world with its own language, customs, and cast of characters. Among the bustling crew members darting about with walkie-talkies, clipboards, and headsets, there's one figure who stands out, not just for their commanding voice but for their uncanny ability to keep everything moving smoothly. This is the First Assistant Director, or First AD, whose role is as essential as coffee on a chilly morning shoot.

Imagine you're hosting a huge party, but instead of guests, you have camera operators, actors, grips, lighting techs, and a director with an ever-changing vision. The First AD is the ultimate event planner, but their "event" is the daily shoot, and their challenge is to ensure it all goes off without a hitch. They're the person charged with keeping everyone on track, ensuring the director's creative ideas become practical actions, and preventing the production from losing precious time or money.

While some people jokingly compare the First AD's job to herding cattle, the reality is much more complex. The First AD is the organizational powerhouse behind the scenes, the voice that rings out above the din to signal that it's time to quiet down, get ready, and make movie magic. Their organizational skills are truly vital. Without a competent First AD, a set can easily descend into chaos, delays, and frustration.

You might hear people say the First AD acts as a gatekeeper for the director, and there's some truth to that. The First AD is usually the buffer between the director and the rest of the crew, translating the director's creative whims and grand ideas into actual, actionable instructions for everyone else. If the director devises a last-minute change in the shot or a fresh approach to a scene, it's the First AD who ensures that everyone is aware of what's happening and what needs to be done. They help shape the director's vision into a workable reality, ensuring that creativity doesn't get bogged down by logistical hurdles.

Let's talk about the First AD's voice. If you've ever watched behind-the-scenes footage, you've probably heard someone shout, "Quiet on set!" or "Rolling!" That's almost certainly the First AD, using their signature, often booming voice to command attention and signal the start of key moments. They're responsible for calling for action, announcing when the crew should be ready, and ensuring that the sound and camera teams are rolling at precisely the right time. When the primary camera is about to capture a scene, it's the First AD who orchestrates all the moving parts, making sure everyone is in sync.

But the duties of a First AD go far beyond just shouting orders. Here are some of the other responsibilities that fall on their shoulders:

- Announcing which department the production is waiting on: Sometimes, the schedule gets delayed because one department, such as maybe lighting or wardrobe, needs a few more minutes. The First AD keeps everyone informed, so there's no confusion about where the holdup is.
- Calling for quiet on the set: Film sets can be noisy places, with people chatting, equipment being moved, and general hustle and bustle. Before the cameras roll, the First AD ensures that absolute silence reigns so that the sound team can capture the best possible audio.
- Clearing the production area of bystanders and non-essential personnel: Strangers or extra crew hanging around can not only be distracting but can also

compromise the shot. The First AD makes sure only those who need to be in the area are present.

• Making sure the production is progressing according to the shooting schedule: Time is money in filmmaking, and falling behind can have serious consequences. The First AD keeps a close eye on the schedule, pushing the crew to stay on track and sometimes making tough calls to keep things moving.

• Directing extras and scene changes: Extras add life to scenes, but they need direction to know where to stand, when to move, and how to behave. The First AD helps coordinate these background performers and ensures that transitions between scenes happen smoothly.

• Scouting for locations: Before shooting can begin, the First AD is often involved in finding suitable locations that meet the director's vision and the practical needs of the production.

• Coordinating the activities of the Line Producer: The Line Producer handles the budget and logistics, while the First AD ensures that these plans are put into action on the day of the shoot. Working together, they're the duo that translates big-picture planning into everyday reality.

Let's imagine a typical day on set. The cast and crew arrive early, and everyone immediately looks to the First AD for instructions. They might start by running through the day's shoot schedule, ensuring everyone knows what scenes will be filmed, when lunch is scheduled, and when key breaks will occur. Throughout the day, they keep everyone focused, troubleshoot problems, and serve as the hub of communication. If a scene is delayed, the First AD makes sure everyone knows why and what's being done to fix it. If an actor needs to be in makeup, if a location requires preparation, or if an extra needs coaching, the First AD orchestrates these details seamlessly.

The role requires a unique combination of interpersonal skills, authority, and in-depth knowledge of filmmaking. A great First AD is diplomatic but firm, approachable but able to command respect, and always thinking several steps ahead. They must anticipate problems before they arise, juggle multiple tasks simultaneously, and manage the needs of a large and diverse team.

In addition to all these duties, the First AD is also the heartbeat of the set's safety culture. They're responsible for ensuring that everyone follows safety protocols, that emergency procedures are in place, and that the crew works in a secure environment. Whether it's crowd control, weather hazards, or keeping the set clear of trip hazards, the First

If you're dreaming of working in film or want to understand how your favourite movies come together, the First AD is a role worth knowing. They're the person who bridges the gap between creativity and practicality, helping turn wild ideas into finished scenes. They're a mix of coach, manager, and referee, keeping the energy high and the chaos at bay.

Ultimately, the First Assistant Director is the glue that holds the production together. Without their steady hand and sharp mind, even the most brilliant director would struggle to bring their vision to life. So, the next time you watch a film, remember that there's someone behind the scenes making sure every moment runs like clockwork. Someone who's catering to the needs of the crew, wrangling the schedule, and making movie magic happen one call for action at a time.

CHAPTER 17

Roles of the Line Producer and Production Coordinator

When most people imagine a film set, they might picture a bustling hive of creative energy—directors shouting "action," camera operators rolling film, and actors delivering lines under the bright glare of studio lights. However, what often goes unnoticed is the intricate, logistical dance that occurs in the background, a dance orchestrated by two of the most crucial yet underappreciated roles in filmmaking: the line producer and the production coordinator.

On smaller projects, these roles may be merged or even blended with other responsibilities; however, on larger productions, the line producer and production coordinator are the backbone of organization and efficiency. Without them, the whole operation can quickly devolve into chaos. Let's take a closer look at what these unsung heroes do and why they're so crucial to the success of any film.

Key Responsibilities of the Line Producer

• Script Distribution: One of the first tasks is ensuring that everyone who needs a copy of the script has one. This doesn't just mean the actors. Camera crews, lighting technicians, art department—everyone needs to be on the same page, literally and figuratively.

• Budget Management: The line producer is central to creating, managing, and sometimes even enforcing the budget. They're the ones who say, "We can't afford another fog machine," or "We need to find a cheaper location for that chase scene." They're the keepers of the purse strings, balancing the director's dreams with financial reality.

• Staffing: Need to hire a last-minute boom operator or find a reliable security guard for the night shoot? That's the line producer's department. They handle the logistics of bringing on additional crew members, sometimes with only hours to spare before the cameras roll.

• Catering and Craft Services: Hungry crew members aren't happy crew members. The line producer coordinates with catering teams or arranges for food delivery and snacks to keep everyone fueled and focused.

• Parking and Logistics: Ever tried to park a fleet of trucks on a busy city street or secure enough spaces for cast, crew, and equipment near a remote country location? The line producer manages the strategic puzzle of parking so that no one's left dragging lights a mile down the road.

• Wardrobe Wrangling: Last-minute costume emergencies? The line producer might be the one hunting down a replacement tuxedo or ironing shirts before a big scene.

• Permits and Legal Paperwork: Shooting in public? You'll need permits. Using a song in your film? That requires paperwork, too. The line producer handles all the legalities, ensuring the production doesn't get shut down by city officials or copyright holders.

• Emergency Supply Runs: When someone realizes at the eleventh hour that you're out of batteries or rain ponchos, the line producer is often the one who dashes out to the nearest store, credit card in hand.

• Release Forms: Every person on camera and every location needs to be cleared legally. The line producer manages the distribution, collection, and filing of these forms, ensuring everything is in order.

- General Go-To Person: Whether it's making phone calls, copying call sheets, or finding a lost prop, the line producer is the person everyone turns to when something needs to be done, especially when time is short.
- Equipment Oversight: Renting gear? The line producer tracks it all, ensuring equipment is returned promptly and in the same condition it left. Lost or damaged equipment can result in costly fees, so careful management is essential.

The Production Coordinator: The Line Producer's Right Hand

If the line producer is the general, the production coordinator is the trusted lieutenant. The coordinator is often in the trenches, managing day-to-day office work and ensuring each department has what it needs. While the line producer oversees the bigger picture, the coordinator handles many of the more minor details that keep things running smoothly.

The production coordinator is often the point of contact for everyone on the crew. Do you need to know where to park tomorrow? Wondering when the call time is? Lost your per diem envelope? Ask the coordinator. They're the hub through which information flows.

Tasks Handled by the Production Coordinator

- Paperwork Central: The coordinator handles a mountain of paperwork: call sheets, production reports, schedules, and release forms. They ensure that documents are copied, distributed, and stored safely for future reference.
- Communication: Information changes fast on a film set. Locations change, times shift, and actors fall ill. The coordinator is responsible for disseminating updates to the relevant parties promptly, typically via phone, email, or mass text messages.

- Emergency Support: When something unexpected comes up, the coordinator is often the one running out for last-minute supplies or finding creative solutions on the fly.
- Logistics Management: Coordinators help arrange transportation, accommodations, and travel for out-of-town cast or crew. They ensure that everyone arrives at their destination on time, with their luggage.

Why These Roles Matter

While the glitz and glamour of filmmaking tend to gravitate toward directors and stars, productions would grind to a halt without the tireless efforts of line producers and production coordinators. They're the problem-solvers, the organizers, and the fixers. When things go wrong, and they always do, these are the people who find a way to keep the show on the road.

On smaller projects, one person may juggle all of these responsibilities simultaneously. On bigger sets, it's a team effort, with each person specializing in a few aspects of this vast logistical puzzle. Either way, their work is crucial to bringing creative ideas to cinematic reality.

In short, the line producer and production coordinator may not have their names in lights, but they're the glue that holds the entire production together. Without them, all the creativity in the world would be for nothing, lost amid a sea of missed deadlines, lost scripts, and hungry, disgruntled crew members. So, the next time you watch a film, spare a thought for the folks in the office trailer. Because without them, there would be no movie to watch at all.

CHAPTER 18

The Script Supervisor

When you dive into the world of filmmaking, you'll quickly discover that the process is rarely as straightforward as simply shooting scene after scene in the order they appear in the script. Most productions shoot out of sequence, jumping from one part of the story to another for reasons ranging from actor availability to location scheduling and weather conditions. This can make keeping track of where your characters are—emotionally, physically, and story-wise—an absolute headache. That's where the script supervisor comes in.

Let's break down what this job is, why it's essential, and how it works on set. If you're planning a shoot or thinking about working in the film industry, understanding the script supervisor's responsibilities will make your production smoother and your finished movie more professional.

What Does a Script Supervisor Actually Do?

At its core, the script supervisor is the guardian of continuity. This means they keep a watchful eye on everything that happens on camera and ensure it all aligns with the script from scene to scene, even when the scenes are shot days or weeks apart.

Think about this: Imagine your lead actor is sporting a red tie in a scene that takes place midway through the story. Then, weeks later, you shoot a scene that's supposed to happen immediately before that, but someone forgets about the tie and it's suddenly missing.

The audience will notice, and it'll break the magic of your film. Continuity errors are distracting, and while some may seem minor, they can add up quickly.

Script supervisors track these details relentlessly. They keep notes on costumes, props, lighting setups, character positions, emotional tone, weather, and even things like the number of sips a character takes from a coffee cup in a scene. Their notes are meticulous, allowing you to match everything up when you come back to shoot additional coverage or pickup shots later.

Why Shooting Out of Sequence Makes the Script Supervisor Crucial

It's almost a given that you'll be shooting scenes out of order. Rarely does a shoot run linearly from the first scene to the last. Maybe your location is only available for a few days, or a key actor has a scheduling conflict that forces you to film their scenes all at once, regardless of where those moments fall in the script.

In these situations, the script supervisor is the person who knows exactly what's happening in the story at any given moment. They know where the characters just came from, where they're going next, and what emotional state they should be in between. This helps the director maintain the emotional arc and ensures the actors don't deliver lines with the wrong energy or expression.

Directors and crew members are often so busy worrying about lighting, camera angles, and the perfect take that they don't have time to refer to the script constantly. The script supervisor acts as the on-set memory bank, ensuring scenes fit together smoothly when edited down the line.

Day One vs. The Rest of the Shoot

You might be able to survive without a script supervisor on the first day, especially if you're only shooting simple scenes in order and everything's fresh. But the minute your production goes out of sequence, even just a little, you'll realize how valuable this role is. It's incredibly easy for continuity mistakes to slip through the cracks once the shoot gets rolling and schedules get complicated.

Even minor discrepancies can become major headaches in post-production. Imagine spending hours searching for footage that matches up, only to discover a wardrobe inconsistency or a missed prop that can't be fixed without a costly reshoot. The script supervisor prevents these issues before they happen, saving time and stress.

Script Supervisor and Clapper Loader

On larger shoots, the script supervisor's role might overlap with that of the clapper loader. The clapper loader is the person who handles the slate, the board flashed in front of the camera at the beginning of each take, which shows the scene and take number. This information is recorded both visually and often audibly, helping editors synchronize audio and video files during post-production.

The slate must match what's being shot. If the numbers or scene information are off, editing becomes a nightmare. Editors must sift through hours of footage to match up takes, which involves additional work and potential confusion. When the script supervisor is also responsible for managing the slate, it ensures a single person is tracking both continuity and scene organization, keeping everything streamlined.

The Slate

If you've ever watched behind-the-scenes footage, you've likely seen someone snap the clapperboard shut, call out the scene and take a number. This isn't just for show. That simple action serves a crucial purpose: it helps the editor line up audio and video, and it marks exactly where each scene and take begins.

When the slate info is wrong, or doesn't match what's happening in the scene, it can take hours, and sometimes days, for editors to figure out which footage goes where. That's time and money wasted. If you want your film to flow smoothly from production to post-production, the person running the slate must be organized and detail-oriented. The script supervisor, with their dedication to accuracy, is the perfect fit.

Script Supervisors in Action

So how does a script supervisor keep up with all this? Here are some of their typical tools and practices:

- Script breakdowns: They mark up the script ahead of time, highlighting costume changes, prop usage, and emotional beats.
- Scene-by-scene notes: On set, they jot down detailed notes for each take, including dialogue variations, actor movements, background details, and more.
- Photo references: Many script supervisors take continuity photos to help match scenes shot on different days.
- Collaboration: They communicate constantly with directors, actors, camera crew, and wardrobe to make sure everyone's on the same page.
- Slate management: When responsible for the slate, they double-check numbers and scene info before every take.

A script supervisor's kit may include binders, highlighters, a camera, and a laptop loaded with continuity software. They're constantly updating their notes, cross-referencing what's been shot, and making sure nothing slips through.

Why You Shouldn't Skip This Role

Some productions, especially low-budget or student films, might think they can get by without a script supervisor. But even on a tight schedule with limited resources, this role pays for itself in saved time, money, and frustration. Continuity errors not only distract viewers, but they can also damage your film's reputation and professional polish.

When your editing team sits down to assemble your footage, they'll thank you for the script supervisor's notes. The process will go faster, smoother, and with fewer unpleasant surprises. Your finished product will feel cohesive, with every scene fitting together as intended.

Final Thoughts

The script supervisor is the unsung hero of the film set. By taking on the responsibility of continuity, scene tracking, and slate management, they allow everyone else, including the director, to focus on creative decisions and performance. Whether they're working solo or combining duties with the clapper loader, their attention to detail and organizational skills make them indispensable.

If you're embarking on a film project, don't overlook this role. Hire a script supervisor or train someone to take on the task. Your future self and your audience will thank you when your film comes together seamlessly, free from distracting mistakes and confusion.

CHAPTER 19

Your Role as Director

Let's be real: being the director isn't just about calling "Action!" and "Cut!" It's about being the guiding force behind what unfolds on set, the person everyone turns to for answers and clarity. The director is, in every sense, the architect of the film's vision. Whether you're crafting a big-budget feature or wrangling talent for a passion project with pocket change, your job is to ensure that what's captured on camera matches the world you've imagined, and that you can bring everyone along for the ride.

The role comes with a fascinating mix of authority and responsibility. Not only are you the person who makes the final call on creative decisions, but you're also the one who, in many cases, is working with a team that's volunteering their time or working for a fraction of what they'd earn elsewhere. This means you have to wear two hats: one as the creative head honcho and another as the resident diplomat, making sure that the energy on set is positive and collaborative. People are far more willing to go the extra mile for you if you're respectful, approachable, and appreciative.

Being Present and Prioritizing

One of the cardinal rules of directing: be on set. If you're not physically present, it isn't easy to steer the ship, and things can drift off course before you know it. There will always be administrative tasks and unexpected fires to put out, but unless something truly urgent pulls you away, your place is with the cast and crew, watching the magic unfold and steering it as needed.

If a task must be handled off-set, delegate it to a reliable assistant or crew member who can take care of the issue and report back. But let's face it, sometimes you don't have a whole team of assistants. In that case, it's essential to master the art of prioritization. Focus on what absolutely requires your attention and maximize your on-set time. When you're present and engaged, you're able to answer questions, approve setups, and maintain momentum.

Directors are the ultimate decision-makers. Lighting, camera angles, blocking, costume tweaks. None of these move forward without your sign-off. This might sound overwhelming, but being the "last word" is what ensures consistency and unity in your film's style and tone. Your crew will look to you for direction, and your input is what turns a collection of talented individuals into a cohesive filmmaking machine.

Handling the Little Things

Directing isn't all about grand creative gestures. Sometimes, it's about the small, practical details that make a shoot run smoothly. You'll likely find yourself:

- Calling for lunch and breaks—keeping the team energized and on schedule.
- Making script tweaks on the fly—streamlining dialogue or adapting to last-minute changes.
- Interfacing with your first Assistant Director (AD)—maintaining the schedule and troubleshooting problems.
- Setting the pace—calling "Action!" at the start of a scene and "Cut!" at the end.

Each of these tasks helps maintain the rhythm of the day, ensuring that everyone is aware of what's happening and feels cared for. It's about striking a balance between creative leadership and practical management.

The Art of Directing Actors

One of the most rewarding (and sometimes challenging) parts of directing is working with actors. They're the face of your story, and getting the best performance out of them is a skill worth honing. There's no shortage of resources on this topic. Judith Weston's "Directing Actors" is a classic for a reason, offering deep insight into the art and craft of guiding performances.

Your main job isn't to tell actors "feel sad now" or "be angry here." Instead, you're the interpreter of character, providing background, motivation, and context. When you share your understanding of a character's journey, you empower actors to bring their own creativity and nuance to the role. This collaborative approach typically yields richer, more authentic performances.

Marking Movement and Blocking

On the technical side, there's the matter of blocking. This is where actors stand, how they move, and what they interact with. If a character's feet are out of frame, a simple piece of tape on the floor can mark their spot. For wider shots, you'll need to rehearse movements to make sure everything looks natural and stays within the frame, avoiding any accidental appearances of tape or equipment.

Rehearsals: Dry and On Camera

Rehearsals are essential. Schedule a "dry" rehearsal a few days before filming, allowing actors to walk through their scenes without the cameras rolling. On shoot day, run quick rehearsals on camera before recording. This fine-tunes blocking, timing, and ensures the actors know exactly where to stand, move, and how to position their hands and heads. It may seem like overkill, but preparation pays off, especially when nerves and adrenaline are at their highest.

Focus Your Attention

A lot is happening on set, and it's easy to get distracted. One tip: keep your eyes on your monitor or viewfinder as much as possible.

Comparing live action to the footage being captured can be confusing, and what you see with your eyes may not match what's recorded. Trust the monitor. It's your window into the final product.

Capturing the Footage You Need

A universal truth in film production: always shoot more than you think you'll need. If you feel three takes are enough, shoot six. Countless variables can render a shot unusable. Lighting shifts, audio glitches, subtle changes in performance. By overshooting, you give yourself options in the editing room, where those extra takes often save the day.

Relaxing the Talent

Actors can get tense, especially in emotionally charged or technically complex scenes. Here's a little trick: sometimes it helps to tell them the camera isn't rolling when it is. This small fib can help them relax and slip into a more natural performance, free from the pressure of "this is the real take."

How Many Takes is Enough?

At a minimum, plan for at least three takes of each item before proceeding. Complicated scenes may require ten, fifteen, or even twenty takes to get it right. Don't feel guilty about asking for repeats. Your goal is to get it right, not to rush the process. The crew and actors may groan, but everyone understands that excellence takes persistence.

Watch Out for Details

Details matter. Keep a keen eye out for reflections in windows and mirrors, stray tire tracks, continuity errors (such as a coffee cup moving between shots), and other minor mistakes that seem insignificant on set but become glaring in post-production. If a scene feels prone to trouble, shoot a few extra takes for safety. It's a simple way to protect yourself from headaches in the future.

Monitoring Takes and Collaborating with Your Crew

If you have a Director of Photography (DP), you'll spend much of your time behind a remote monitor, watching the feed as it comes in. It's rare to peer through the camera itself. Your monitor shows you exactly what's being captured. Still, it's smart to occasionally check with your DP to confirm that the monitor and camera views match, catching any technical issues early.

When shooting on film (as opposed to digital), you'll use a viewfinder: a small device that's adjusted for the aspect ratio you're shooting in. Whether you're planning for standard TV, cinematic widescreen, or something in between, you need to make this decision before production begins. The viewfinder allows you to frame shots precisely, and while some directors bring their own, it's a handy tool for any director. If you're in a pinch, you can even improvise with a piece of cardboard cut to the correct size or your hands held up in a frame.

Gear Tips

You don't need to spend a fortune on equipment. A used viewfinder costs as little as $100 and is helpful for any medium. The key is to prioritize tools that help you visualize your shots and communicate clearly with your camera crew. Technology evolves, but a director's need to see exactly what's being captured never changes.

Knowing When to Call It a Wrap

This is one of those moments that separates good directors from great ones. You've lived with this film in your mind for weeks, months, maybe even years. You know every shot, every beat, every nuance. When the time comes, trust your instincts. You'll know when you've got what you need.

Of course, your crew will offer feedback and suggestions. Sometimes, you'll get helpful ideas for adjusting a take or approaching a scene in a different way. Listen to them but remember: the final decision rests with you. It's your film, your vision.

The Shooting Schedule Factor

Your schedule is important. You'll need to capture all the essential shots, but there's an art to deciding when you have enough. The coverage that allows you to build the film in editing without unnecessary gaps. When you look at your script, your storyboards, and your notes, and see that you've checked off every critical moment, it's time to call "wrap."

A Well-Earned Wrap Party

Few things are as satisfying as wrapping a shoot. Cast and crew love it; it's a chance to celebrate, unwind, and recognize everyone's hard work. Take the opportunity to express your gratitude. A simple "thank you" goes a long way, but if you want to really mark the occasion, host a wrap party. Your team will appreciate knowing that their efforts mattered and that you value their contribution.

There's a practical side, too. At the wrap party, share a rough timeline for when everyone can see the finished film. Keep them in the loop. It builds anticipation and fosters a sense of community.

Sharing Production Stills and Memories

If you've captured production stills (behind-the-scenes photos), share them as soon as you can. In the digital age, this is easier than ever. Send them out via email, social media, or any other preferred platform. These images give your cast and crew something to show off to friends and family while they wait for the final cut. It's also a great way to keep the buzz alive as you move into post-production.

Distributing the Final Cut

When your film is finished and ready for distribution, whether that's at festivals, streaming, or a private screening, ensure that everyone who worked on it receives a copy. It's a gesture that shows respect and appreciation, and it lets your collaborators share in the pride of a well-done project.

The Director's Journey

Directing is a blend of vision, management, artistic leadership, and a good dose of grit. You'll spend days making tough decisions, guiding performances, troubleshooting technical issues, and maintaining high morale. It's not always glamorous, and sometimes you'll feel stretched thin trying to juggle everything. But when you watch your film come together, from rough cut to final edit, you'll know every ounce of effort was worth it.

Remember that no two sets or films are the same. Each project brings its own set of challenges and surprises, but the fundamentals stay constant: be present, communicate clearly, support your team, and always keep your eyes on the story you set out to tell.

If you can do that with a good dose of humility, confidence, and adaptability, you'll not only survive as a director, but you'll also thrive. And you'll inspire those around you to do their best work, bringing your collective vision to life for audiences to enjoy.

Whether you're prepping for your first short film or gearing up for a feature, keep these principles in mind. Lead with empathy, make decisions boldly, and cherish every step of the filmmaking journey. The stories we tell, and the teams we build, are what make directing such a rewarding adventure.

PART 4

POST-PRODUCTION

CHAPTER 20

Editing

Editing isn't just a technical necessity. It's the thrilling, sometimes daunting, stage where your film finally starts to take the shape you imagined all along. After all the planning, prepping, sweating through takes, and calling "Cut!" more times than you can count, post-production is where all those pieces—scenes, shots, sounds—get stitched, welded, and coaxed into a coherent, captivating whole. If you've never sat down in an editing bay before, prepare yourself: it can be a marathon, not a sprint. However, it's also, for many filmmakers, the most rewarding part of the journey, the point where the raw material starts to shine.

Piecing Together the Story

So, you've wrapped up the shoot. Maybe you're looking at hours—sometimes days—of footage, and you're wondering, "Where on earth do I start?" Editing is where you'll make the crucial choices that shape not just what your audience sees, but how they feel about it. Here, you'll comb through your production stills, line up those takes, and select the very best of the bunch. Sometimes, you'll have plenty of options. Other times, especially on indie or low-budget shoots, you might find yourself working with what you've got, even if every shot isn't exactly what you'd dreamed up on set.

One thing to keep in mind from the start: editing can take far longer than the actual filming process. Shooting is often a fast-paced, adrenaline-fueled experience, with the cast and crew bustling from one location to another. But editing? That's where the pace changes. You'll spend hours, maybe days or even weeks, watching, rewatching, and fine-tuning your footage. And unlike the collaborative atmosphere of a film set, editing can be a quieter, more solitary affair. It's just you (or maybe you and your editor), your raw footage, and a mountain of creative decisions.

Working With What You Have

Let's be real: most filmmakers don't have the luxury of endless reshoots. Maybe you're working with a tight budget, limited time, or a cast and crew who are already moving on to their next projects. That means you need to be flexible in the editing room. Didn't get the perfect shot? Sometimes, it's about making the best of what you have.

For instance, say you notice in post that the boom mic has crept into the frame. Don't panic! You can often crop in a bit tighter on your shot. If you aren't cutting off your actors' heads or otherwise ruining the composition, you might find that this new, closer angle is even more compelling than what you'd originally planned. Editing is a lot like problem-solving. It rewards creativity, flexibility, and a willingness to let go of what you thought had to be. And remember, it's usually easier to cut problematic shots from something like a trailer than from a short film, where every moment is precious. Either way, don't be afraid to experiment.

Shaping the Visual Narrative

Film, above all, is a visual medium, and editing is where visual storytelling takes place in earnest. Whether you shot on traditional film or went digital, the editing suite is where you'll start literally piecing your story together.

First, you'll create a rough cut. This is a loose, working version of your film. It's your chance to experiment, to see what works and what doesn't, without getting bogged down in the details. As you watch your raw footage, take notes on your favourite takes, moments, and performances. The rough cut is like a sketch—it doesn't need to be perfect, but it should give you a sense of the film's pacing, structure, and rhythm.

From there, you'll move on to the final cut, where you'll polish and perfect the film. This is when you'll really start to see your vision coming together. Don't rush. Watch and rewatch, try things out, and don't be afraid to make bold choices. Sometimes, the best moments arise from happy accidents or unexpected outcomes.

It's also worth noting that special effects, if you're using them, usually come toward the end of the editing process, after you've locked the rough cut, but before the final polish. This way, you know exactly how the effects will fit into the finished product.

Editing takes time, sometimes a lot of it. Even a short, five-minute trailer can require days of work to get right. If you're working with an editor, make sure you're both on the same page about the timeline, the vision, and the workflow.

Choosing Your Editing Environment

Where you do your editing can have a significant impact on your experience and your film. Some filmmakers work at home, using their own computers and software. Others work with professional "post houses"—dedicated editing studios with state-of-the-art gear and skilled technicians.

Post houses have their perks. You'll get access to high-end software (like Avid or Final Cut Pro), professional editors, and top-notch technical support. If you're working with a post house, you and your editor will sit together, reviewing footage, making cuts, and fine-tuning the film. This environment can help keep you focused and on task, and the expertise of a good editor is invaluable.

One handy tip: it's often a good idea to work with an editor who wasn't present during the shoot. Why? Because as the director, you're probably emotionally invested in every frame. You remember how hard it was to get that sunset shot, or how hilarious that line was on set. However, sometimes footage that seemed crucial during shooting just doesn't serve the story in the edit. A fresh-eyed editor can help you make those tough calls, trimming the fat and focusing on the narrative. They're your first test audience, and their feedback is gold.

Of course, not every filmmaker has the budget for a fancy post house. If you're working on a shoestring, you might be editing at home, maybe even on borrowed software. Be cautious here. Using pirated or borrowed programs can lead to legal issues if your film becomes successful. A better option is to barter or trade for editing services with a friend or local freelancer. Maybe they'll let you use their post house during off-hours in exchange for a credit or a future favour. Just be prepared: their day job (such as handling corporate videos) will take priority if client deadlines conflict.

Regardless of where you edit, strive to be as organized as possible. Before you even start, go through your footage and cut anything that's clearly unusable. If you tried complex in-camera effects or had scenes that required tons of takes, pare down those options so you're only working with the best material. This will save you and your editor a ton of time and energy.

The Final Edit

When you're ready for the final edit, treat your footage like treasure. If you shot on digital video, you could work directly from a copy of the raw material. Always, and this cannot be stressed enough, make backups. Preferably, use a RAID storage device or some other reliable system to safeguard your footage. Data loss can derail a project faster than you can say render error.

If your computer isn't the fastest or most powerful, you might need to work with lower-resolution versions ("proxies") of your footage to keep things running smoothly. Edit with these, and only output the final, high-resolution version when you're ready to export your finished film.

It's standard practice to do your rough cut on your home computer, then move to a post house or a more powerful setup for the final tweaks and output. That way, you're getting the best of both worlds: the comfort and affordability of home editing, plus the professional finish of a studio-grade setup, if your budget allows.

Scripting, Software, and Output Formats

Keep your shooting script handy during editing and make detailed notes as you go. Where you cut, which takes you prefer, any ideas for sound or effects. Most editing software lets you add markers or notes directly onto the timeline, which is a huge help. When you're ready, use the fastest machine you can access to assemble your "online" or full-resolution cut, then output it to your final delivery format, usually a standard DVD, but maybe a digital file if you're sending it to festivals or streaming platforms. Don't forget menus and credits!

Making Every Frame Beautiful

Even if your on-set lighting was flawless, chances are good you'll need to do some colour correction in post. This is where you balance brightness, contrast, and colour tone to ensure the film looks consistent from scene to scene, even if you had to shoot over several days or under different lighting conditions.

With digital footage, colour correction happens in software. With film, you'll transfer your footage to video, make your corrections, and then create a new negative. You can apply colour corrections to the whole movie or just to specific scenes. Sometimes, you'll use a special look or style, such as the famous "bleach bypass" technique, which makes colours look faded and gritty, perfect for noir or war stories.

Good colour correction can be the difference between a film that feels amateur and one that pops off the screen. Use it to enhance mood, unify disparate shots, and add visual interest.

Crafting a Rich Soundscape

Audio is every bit as crucial as visuals when it comes to immersing your audience in the story. Even a well-recorded film will need audio work in post. Maybe you need to add music, sound effects, or even re-record dialogue that didn't come out clean on set.

Music is a biggie. Choosing the correct score (or even composing your own) can elevate a scene from mundane to magical. Sound effects, too, add layers of realism and excitement. And don't be afraid to get creative here. You can use digital filters to modify voices, add atmosphere, or mask technical hiccups.

If you're new to audio, consider working with a sound professional. Many are willing to barter or donate their services in exchange for on-screen credit or a chance to work on a future project. Good audio is an investment that pays off, and a professional touch can be the difference between a film that feels like a student project and one that really sings.

Fine-Tuning Dialogue

No matter how skilled your actors or how careful your sound team, there will almost always be moments when you need to re-record dialogue in post. This process, known as Additional Dialogue Recording (ADR), is usually done in a quiet studio, with your actors looping lines as they watch the footage.

The goal is to minimize ADR as much as possible, since matching new dialogue to the original performance can be challenging. But sometimes you have no choice. Maybe a plane flew overhead during your best take, or an actor flubbed a line in an otherwise perfect shot. ADR lets you patch things up without reshooting.

Another use for ADR is adding brand-new lines to scenes, either to clarify the story, cover up an edit, or add a voice-over (especially handy in trailers). To make ADR sound natural, your sound engineer will record "room tone". This is about 30 seconds of quiet from the filming location used as a base. They'll also do their best to match the microphones and acoustics used on set, so the new dialogue blends seamlessly with the rest.

And don't stress if your actors aren't pros at voice work. For many indie projects, you may end up doing the ADR yourself or recruiting friends to help out. Focus on clarity and matching the emotional tone of the original performance.

The Art of Sound Effects

If you've ever watched a movie and marvelled at how real everything sounds—the footsteps, the rain, the clatter of dishes—that's the magic of foley artists. These behind-the-scenes wizards recreate everyday sounds (and sometimes wild, imaginative ones) to add depth and realism to your film.

Foley is more than just technical trickery; it's an art form. It requires a keen ear, a strong sense of rhythm, and a deep understanding of how sound affects mood and storytelling. Even in the simplest shoots, there's room for foley work, whether it's footsteps, gunfire, rustling leaves, or the background hum of a busy street.

Sometimes, foley is about creating a sense of place. Maybe you shot a restaurant scene in your living room, but you want it to sound like a bustling diner. Layer in some background chatter, the clink of glasses, distant traffic, and voilà! Or perhaps you're filming a suspense scene set inside a bank vault, but your set is just a plywood box. Foley lets you add those deep, metallic reverberations that tell viewers, "This is a vault."

Don't be afraid to get inventive. Foley artists have used everything from coconut shells (for horse hooves) to crinkling cellophane (for fire) to get the right sound. There's no one way to do it. Just experiment and have fun.

Bringing It All Together

Editing is where your film truly comes to life. It's a process that demands patience, flexibility, and a willingness to adapt. You'll make tough decisions, cutting shots you spent hours getting just right, tweaking audio until it's just so, wrestling with software quirks and technical glitches. However, you'll also experience the deep satisfaction that comes from seeing your vision finally come to life.

Remember, there's no one right way to edit a film. Some directors map out every cut before they even shoot. Others discover the story in the editing room, finding new rhythms and meanings in the footage itself. The important thing is to stay open, stay curious, and don't be afraid to try something new.

Whether you're working alone on your laptop or collaborating with a whole post-production team, editing is a journey of discovery. It's where your film grows from a collection of raw moments into something that can move, surprise, and delight an audience. Embrace the process, keep your mind open, and enjoy the ride. After all, when the credits roll and the lights come up, you'll know every frame, every cut, every sound is the result of your hard work and creative vision.

And isn't that what filmmaking is all about?

CHAPTER 21

Output and Distribution

After months (or maybe even years) of hard work—writing, shooting, editing, pouring your heart and soul into your film—at long last, you're done. The final cut is locked, the music is synced up just right, and the credits roll as you envisioned. There's nothing quite like the feeling of seeing your creative vision finally take shape on the screen. But before you pop the champagne and start calling yourself the next big thing in cinema, there's still a crucial hurdle to clear: getting your film out into the world. Welcome to the wild world of output and distribution.

The Test Audience

Before you start thinking about red carpets or distribution deals, pump the brakes for a second. One of the most essential steps, one that can make or break your film's success, is showing your movie to someone who has no prior knowledge of your story, your intentions, or your artistic choices. This fresh eyes approach is invaluable. After spending so much time with your film, you're too close to the material to see it objectively. You know every backstory, every nuance, and every inside joke. But what about someone who's watching for the very first time?

Find a friend or acquaintance with no prior knowledge of your project and let them watch. Don't explain, don't guide, watch their reactions. Afterwards, ask honest questions: Did it make sense?

Were there any confusing moments? Did the emotional beats land as intended? If they're scratching their head or seem lost, don't take it personally. Think of their feedback as a treasure map leading you to a tighter, stronger film. Sometimes, this means returning to the editing room to make changes, cut scenes, or reorder sequences. It's all part of the process, and believe me, your future audience will appreciate it.

Once your test audience gives you a big thumbs-up and you can watch your film without cringing or wanting to fix "just one more thing," you're ready for the next step.

Preparing for Mass Production: Mastering and Duplicating Your Film

Now, let's talk about making copies of your masterpiece. In the old days, this meant sending reels to a lab and hoping nothing got scratched. Nowadays, most filmmakers finish their projects digitally and often distribute their films via DVD, Blu-ray, or digital downloads. If you're going the physical route, you'll need to get your movie professionally "mastered." This means creating a pristine, high-quality version (a master copy) from which all duplicates will be made.

To bulk-duplicate DVDs, you'll typically send your master to a professional mastering house or duplication facility. They'll take care of producing as many copies as you need, whether it's a dozen for family and friends, or hundreds for a festival screening or small theatrical run. Don't forget about the presentation: the packaging, labels, and artwork are all part of the impression you make. Some filmmakers design these themselves using graphic design tools like Photoshop, Canva, or GIMP, giving their project a unique personal touch. If your design skills are lacking, consider recruiting a talented friend or hiring a freelance designer. Remember, people often judge a DVD by its cover.

Who Needs to See Your Film?

You have a stack of DVDs (or a file ready to upload) and you're buzzing with excitement. Now comes a significant question: Who do you want to see your film? Maybe you're dreaming of a packed movie theatre, or perhaps you want industry insiders and potential investors to notice what you've created. No matter your goal, this is where your work shifts from filmmaking to marketing, and it's a whole new ball game.

Getting people to actually watch your film is a challenge that shouldn't be underestimated. Many filmmakers pour all their energy into making the movie and then feel lost when it comes to getting it seen. But distribution is the bridge between your creative work and your audience. Whether you made your film for love, profit, or both, this is the point where you need to don your promoter's hat.

Marketing

Most artists would rather pull an all-nighter editing than spend a day networking. But marketing is the engine that drives your film out of obscurity and into the hands (or screens) of viewers. A huge reason some independent films never find their audience isn't because they're bad, but because their creators didn't do the necessary homework on how to market their work.

Marketing isn't just about booking a slot on a talk show or buying ads. It's about sharing your passion, getting people excited, and building a network. This can mean reaching out in person, sending emails, making phone calls, and connecting through social media. Cultivating genuine relationships with festival programmers, bloggers, reviewers, and even other filmmakers can open doors you didn't even know existed. Yes, it takes time and energy, but your film deserves it.

All About Distribution: Old School vs. New School

Distribution is often the make-or-break phase for a film, and the landscape is constantly evolving. Traditionally, getting your movie into theatres or physical stores meant jumping through a lot of hoops and convincing gatekeepers. While that's still an option, there are now more paths than ever for getting your work out there, especially for independent filmmakers.

- Theatrical Distribution: Still the "holy grail" for many, but also the toughest to crack. You'll need connections, a compelling pitch, and often, a distributor to bring your film to local or national theatres.
- Festivals: Submitting your film to festivals is a time-honoured way to get it in front of both audiences and industry professionals. A strong festival run can build buzz, attract media coverage, and sometimes lead to a distribution deal. Do your research: each festival has its own focus, deadlines, and requirements.
- DVD and Blu-ray Sales: While streaming has taken over much of the market, physical media still has its place, especially as collectibles or for regions where streaming isn't as prevalent. Direct-to-DVD overseas markets can be surprisingly lucrative for specific genres.
- Online Platforms: The rise of direct online distribution has democratized the process. You can sell or rent your film on your own website, or use established platforms like iTunes, Amazon Video, or Vimeo On Demand. These sites handle the transaction and delivery, taking a small cut.
- Specialty Distribution: Don't overlook unique opportunities, such as distributing your film through hotel or airline networks. These channels can expose your work to diverse, captive audiences and sometimes come with attractive licensing deals.

Short Films and Online Sharing

Maybe your project isn't a feature film. Perhaps it's a short, a trailer, or even a web series pilot. The digital world is tailor-made for you! Uploading your content to sites like YouTube, Vimeo, or other niche platforms (like Atom Films or I-Films) can help you reach global audiences with almost no upfront cost. While it's unlikely you'll earn big bucks charging for a short film online, sharing it freely can serve as your calling card to showcase your talent to potential collaborators, festivals, or investors.

If you're hoping to monetize a short film, consider working with touring short film showcases that play in theatres and share ticket proceeds, or entering competitions that offer cash prizes. But even if your short doesn't earn money, the exposure and recognition can open doors. Sometimes, a great short is all it takes to land your next big project.

Film Festivals

Film festivals are more than just screenings—they're networking events, press opportunities, and sometimes, launchpads for careers. Submitting your film to both local and international festivals gives you a shot at awards, reviews, and, most importantly, connections. Pay attention to submission rules, formats, and deadlines, and be strategic about where you send your film. A festival laureate can add credibility to your work and help you create buzz among industry insiders and general audiences alike.

Building Your Audience

Getting your film out there isn't a one-and-done task. Think of distribution and marketing as an ongoing process. Keep in touch with your audience through social media, email newsletters, or behind-the-scenes updates. Encourage viewers to share the film, write reviews, or recommend it to friends. The more you engage with your fans, the more likely they are to support your future projects.

Embrace the Journey

Ultimately, output and distribution are just as creative and challenging as the filmmaking process itself. Don't be discouraged if the road feels long or the results aren't immediate. Every filmmaker, no matter how big, starts somewhere. By putting as much thought and energy into sharing your film as you did into making it, you'll give your work its best chance to shine. So, show your movie to fresh eyes, prepare it with care, and set it free into the world—who knows where it will take you next?

CONCLUSION

5 Tips for Creating Your Best Film: Casual Insights for Aspiring Filmmakers

Making a feature film is no small feat. For most people, the process is daunting, filled with hurdles you might not even anticipate until you're knee-deep in filming. Whether you're an absolute beginner or someone with a few short films under your belt, venturing into the world of feature-length movies brings its own unique set of challenges. The truth is, filmmaking is a delicate balancing act between creativity and logistics, vision and reality. To create a movie that truly stands out, one that captivates your audience and makes you proud, you'll need to pay attention to a handful of key areas.

Below, you'll find five practical tips, each designed to guide you through the major steps of turning your concept into an engaging, polished film. These aren't just technical instructions; they're lessons drawn from experience, aimed at helping you spot potential pitfalls before they turn into major setbacks, and giving you the confidence to tackle each stage with purpose and energy.

1. Crafting an Irresistible Script

Let's start at the very beginning—the script. Your script is more than just words on a page; it's the blueprint, the heart, and the soul of your entire project. Think of it as your film's foundation: if it's shaky, everything else you build upon it risks falling apart. A script that's rushed or underdeveloped can leave actors uninterested, audiences bored, and the whole production feeling flat.

How do you make your script irresistible? Dedicate substantial time to developing your characters. Audiences crave stories they can connect with, and this is only possible when the characters are vivid, relatable, and real. Give each character a backstory, motivations, quirks, and flaws. Make them people your actors can understand, and your audience can emotionally invest in.

If you neglect this aspect, your film may struggle to hold the audience's attention, regardless of its fancy visuals or clever editing tricks. The characters are your audience's way into the world you're creating, so make sure they're worth sticking around for. This also makes your actors' jobs easier; when actors can see the depth and complexity in their roles, they're more likely to bring genuine passion and energy to the performance.

Speaking of actors, be selective in your casting, even if you're working with a limited budget. While you might not have access to Oscar-winning talent, that doesn't mean you can't assemble a committed team. Look for actors who genuinely care about your story and want to contribute to your vision. The difference between a passionate actor and someone who shows up to recite lines is huge. The audience can sense when someone's heart isn't in it, and that disconnect can drag down an otherwise promising movie. Never underestimate the power of good casting. Choose people who fit their roles naturally, and don't force anyone into a part that doesn't suit them.

2. Scheduling and Planning for Reshoots

If you've ever worked on any project with a deadline, you know things rarely go exactly as planned. Film shoots are notorious for unexpected complications—bad weather, broken equipment, scheduling conflicts, and numerous other minor hiccups. That's why it's essential to build a flexible shooting schedule, one that allows for delays and setbacks without derailing the whole production.

Give yourself extra days for possible reshoots, and don't be afraid to overestimate how long things might take. The worst-case scenario is finishing ahead of schedule. Still, if you don't allow enough time, you could find yourself in a situation where you're forced to compromise on quality, or, in the most extreme cases, abandon the project altogether. It's much better to have unused days than to be scrambling in a panic at the end.

Reshoots aren't just about fixing mistakes—they're a safety net. Sometimes, you'll realize in editing that a particular scene doesn't work as well as you hoped, or you'll spot continuity issues that need to be addressed. If you've built enough flexibility into your schedule, these fixes are much less stressful. Ensure that some of your budget is allocated for these inevitable moments. Having a financial cushion for last-minute changes is just as important as setting aside time.

3. Editing in Bite-Sized Chunks

Editing is where the magic happens. Raw footage can be transformed into a compelling narrative, and the choices you make here significantly impact the pacing, tone, and clarity of your film. But editing is also a marathon, not a sprint. Trying to power through all the footage in one go might seem efficient, but it's a recipe for mistakes, burnout, and missed opportunities.

Instead, break the editing process into manageable segments. Tackle one scene or sequence at a time, and give yourself space to review, refine, and rethink as you go. This approach keeps your mind fresh and your judgment sharp, so you're less likely to overlook problems or let fatigue cloud your creative decisions.

If possible, step away from the project for a few days after the shoot before jumping into editing. Coming back with a fresh perspective can lead to better, more honest evaluations of what works and what doesn't. You'll spot things you might have missed in the heat of the moment, and you'll be better equipped to make cuts and changes that ultimately serve the story.

4. Seeking Feedback Before Distribution

Finishing your film is incredibly rewarding, but before you rush to share it with the world, take time to gather feedback. This can be nerve-wracking. No one likes hearing criticism about something they've poured their heart and soul into. However, it's a crucial step in ensuring your movie resonates with viewers.

Show your film to a trusted group of friends, family, or fellow filmmakers, and be open to their constructive feedback and opinions. Not all feedback will be helpful, but distinguishing between personal preferences and substantive issues is key. For instance, if someone points out that a plot point is confusing, that's worth addressing. If the critique is about a character's hair colour or wardrobe, something rooted in personal taste, you can take it or leave it.

Try not to take criticism personally. Even the best films go through rounds of revisions and tough notes. The goal is to make your story as strong as possible, and outside perspectives can highlight weaknesses you might not see in yourself. Use this input constructively, refining your film so it's polished and engaging for a wider audience.

5. Enlisting Help from Friends and Family

There's a common misconception that filmmaking is a solitary pursuit. It's one of the most collaborative art forms out there. Don't hesitate to reach out to your network for help. Friends, family, and acquaintances might be excited to contribute, whether by lending equipment, providing a location, or just helping out on set.

Even if they don't have direct experience in film, your supporters can offer valuable perspectives, resources, and encouragement. Sometimes, a single connection can introduce you to someone with specialized skills, or point you toward funding sources you hadn't considered. Building a community around your project makes the journey more fun and increases your chances of success.

This collaborative spirit can be the difference between a stalled idea and a completed film. So, tap into your network, share your vision, and invite others to join the adventure. You never know who might be able to help get your project off the ground.

Go Make Something Incredible!

Creating a feature film is a bold and ambitious undertaking, marked by challenges and rich learning experiences. By focusing on the script, allowing for reshoots, taking a thoughtful approach to editing, welcoming honest feedback, and embracing the support of your community, you're giving yourself the best possible chance to produce a movie that stands out.

Don't be afraid to experiment, make mistakes, and learn as you go. The process can be unpredictable, sometimes frustrating, but always rewarding. So gather your ideas, rally your team, and start bringing your vision to life. The world is waiting to see what you create. Now go out and make something amazing!

A FINAL NOTE FROM THE AUTHOR

Thank you for reading my book. I hope you found some of it useful. If you enjoyed it, or found any tips helpful, please take a moment to leave a review at the online retailer you purchased it from.

If you find any errors, or if you have any additional tips or info that you feel should be added, please contact me.

Thanks,

Liane Mahugh
Nanaimo, BC

Scan the QR code to see other books by Liane Mahugh.

ABOUT THE AUTHOR

LIANE MAHUGH

Liane lives on Vancouver Island, in Western Canada, with her two sons and their mini-Yorkie. She spends a lot of her spare time exploring museums with her youngest son and talking to the dog. Why? Because the dog is an attentive listener and never talks back.

You can find her on Facebook, Bluesky, and Instagram. Visit her website to sign up for her mailing list and find more info about her books.

Website: www.lianemahugh.ca/books
Instagram: https://www.instagram.com/lianemahugh
Bluesky: Liane Mahugh @halffulllibrary.bsky.social
Facebook: www.facebook.com/writingincanada